More Picture Book Story Hours

From Parties to Pets

Paula Gaj Sitarz

Libraries Unlimited, Inc.
Englewood, Colorado
1990

LIBRARIES UNLIMITED, INC.
P.O. Box 3988
Englewood, Colorado 80155-3988

Library of Congress Cataloging-in-Publication Data

Sitarz, Paula Gaj, 1955-
   More picture book story hours : from parties to pets / Paula Gaj Sitarz.
   xii, 166 p. 17x25 cm.
   Includes bibliographical references.
   ISBN 0-87287-764-7
   1. Libraries, Children's--Activity programs. 2. Children--Books and reading. 3. Picture-books for children. 4. Storytelling.
I. Title.
Z718.3.S58   1990
027.62'51--dc20   89-78336
                                        CIP

To Michael, Andrew, Kate, and Dad

Contents

THE PROGRAM PLANS

Acknowledgments

I am grateful to the children's staff of the New Bedford Free Public Library, New Bedford, Massachusetts, and to the staffs of the North Dartmouth Library, North Dartmouth, Massachusetts, and the Southworth Library, South Dartmouth, Massachusetts, for their assistance.

Introduction

"This is my first year doing story hour. What works?"

"I don't have much time to plan story hour. What should I do?"

"Do preschoolers enjoy a story hour on hats?"

"I'm bored with this program outline. There must be another way to do a story hour on rainy days."

"Sure, I'll do story hour while you're on vacation. Just leave a program plan."

Sound familiar?

If you're doing story hours for the first time ...

If you have little time to prepare programs ...

If you're afraid to try an untested program plan ...

If you'd like to present a program subject in a new way ...

If you're asked to do a story hour for someone ...

The story-hour program plans in this book will help.

For six years I enjoyed doing story hours with four- and five-year-old youngsters at the Thomas Crane Public Library in Quincy, Massachusetts. I worked with many groups of preschoolers: those who attended the picture book story hour which runs from October to May; those who attended summer programs; and those who visited from nursery and preschools. Successful stories and activities remained in my repertoire. Less successful stories and activities were dropped.

I tried various formats, explored many story-hour subjects, and consulted other experienced children's librarians. I spent hours searching shelves, consulting professional resources, thumbing through card catalogs, and hunting down books in other libraries. I agonized over whether the children would enjoy a certain story or activity and if the order in which I presented the material would work.

The result of these efforts is the twenty-two tested story-hour program plans you find in this book. They are easy to do and in most cases involve no cost. As for running time: everyone reads at a different pace, of course, and audience participation definitely impacts time, but in general the programs outlined here take between thirty and forty-five minutes each.

The first chapter, "Putting It Together," is a guide to selecting, organizing, preparing, executing, and evaluating material for story hours. You'll also find information about location and space requirements, registration, publicity, and programs for parents.

Each program plan is preceded by publicity ideas. If you're doing a series of programs, you won't need to publicize each one, but if you use any of these programs during the summer or during a vacation week, then you might want to publicize it individually.

Within each program plan, you'll find: ways to introduce your read alouds and other material; actual book talks that vary in length; and suggestions on how to use other material in the program. Fingerplays and action rhymes are reprinted in the program plans. The plans are followed by "Try This!", a selective list of other books to read aloud and other material options: book talks, other story forms, poetry, participation books, fingerplays and action rhymes, songs, filmstrips, films, and activities. Full bibliographic information is given for each item, and I've indicated whether a title is wordless or nonfiction or if it works well as a felt-board story.

The final chapter, "Resources and Aids," is an annotated list of books that will also help you plan and execute your programs.

Out-of-print books, as well as books in print, are included in the text because most library collections have a good selection of both. Books also go out of print at a moment's notice, and they can just as quickly be reissued or reprinted. If a title is not readily available, request it from another library.

Use the program plans as are, or use them as a starting point, a springboard to adapt to your particular needs. Modify the plans using your own ideas or using some of the other materials suggested for each topic. Delete, alter, lengthen, shorten, or rearrange as needed. If you have three year olds in your story hour, substitute some of the shorter book titles listed in "Try This!"

Whether the topic is bathtime, bedtime, or birds, you're sure to find a subject in the pages that follow to please those eager preschoolers!

Putting
It Together

SELECTING MATERIAL

Do you remember when your English teacher gave you an assignment to write a report? If the teacher didn't suggest a topic, you agonized over what you should write. The same is true when planning story hours. It's difficult to decide what unrelated material to put together. Instead, think of books you feel are worth sharing and group them by subject. Don't pick too narrow a topic, though. If you do, you might end up using some titles of inferior quality merely because you need material to fit your subject.

Select topics that interest and are within the understanding of children ages four and five. Ideal subjects include the family, friends, seasons, food, colors, holidays, and animals.

The main goals of the story hour are to bring children's literature of artistic and literary merit to youngsters and to have children view books and reading as pleasurable experiences. Thus, reading aloud is the focus of the picture book story hour.

The only way to find appropriate books to read aloud is to read widely, from several library collections. Use published book lists, retrospective and current, to point you toward good titles. Review sources keep you abreast of what's being published and help you eliminate titles not worth considering. The primary journals are *School Library Journal, The Horn Book, Kirkus Reviews, Booklist,* and *Bulletin of the Center for Children's Books.* But these lists and journals are only a starting point. To know if a title will work, you must read it aloud several times.

Look for books with a straightforward story line that can be absorbed in one listening. A good read aloud has pleasing language and is satisfying in some way. The illustrations are a prime consideration. Can they be seen and appreciated by a group? Are the illustrations distinct and uncluttered? Do they enhance the text or distract from it? Are the illustrations appropriately placed? It's confusing and frustrating to children if you're talking about a boy who discovers a magic box, and they don't see the accompanying visual until you turn the page.

Several types of books work well with preschoolers. John Burningham's *Mr. Gumpy's Outing* is an example of a cumulative story. Each action builds on the one before to an inevitable climax. Mr. Gumpy invites numerous animals and two children for a ride in his boat. He tells each character to behave in a certain way; they don't and the boat tips over. They all swim to shore and have tea together. The book also has distinctive characters; swift plotting; and a clear beginning, middle, and end.

The *Three Billy Goats Gruff,* written by P.C. Asbjornsen and illustrated by Marcia Brown, features repetition of action and language. Most folktales share this quality. The three billy goats must cross a bridge beneath which lives a mean troll. Each goat "trip traps" over the bridge, and each is threatened by the troll. The setting, characters, and conflict are established quickly, and once the climax arrives, the ending comes swiftly. Folktales are an excellent choice for story hour because they are meant to be read or told aloud.

In *The Snowy Day,* Ezra Jack Keats evokes a mood. Children can join Peter on his adventures in the city on a snowy day. The words are carefully chosen; the colors are bold and vibrant. The mood is one of joy with nature.

Children also like stories that have a character with whom they can identify. In *Happy Birthday, Sam* by Pat Hutchins, Sam thinks that a birthday means he can suddenly do things he couldn't do before.

Also share stories that have a character who is in a situation or who exhibits an emotion with which children can identify. Check out *Dogger* by Shirley Hughes in which David loses his beloved stuffed animal.

The story hour brings together children with different interests, tastes, and ranges of experience, so provide stories with various themes or treatments of a single theme and stories with varying plots, characters, settings, tempos, and artistic qualities. Use books that will stretch the imagination, make children curious and satisfy their curiosity, tell them something about the world in a familiar or new way, or make them laugh. Make a special effort to use well-written books with female characters in the main role. These are still difficult to find for this age group.

You'll want to share books that are well executed in terms of style, content, format, and packaging. Consequently, hardcover books are generally preferable to paperback editions.

Never assume that children have heard the "classics," i.e., *The Three Little Pigs, Angus and the Ducks* by Majorie Flack, or *Where the Wild Things Are* by Maurice Sendak. They might not have. And, even if they have, children like to hear a good story again and again. If a story fits into several program subjects, use it more than once in different ways — as a book talk, a read aloud, or a felt-board story. Share different interpretations of the same story — different retellings, different illustrations, or both.

Ultimately, the most important consideration in choosing stories to read aloud is to select stories that you like and which interest you. You can't generate enthusiasm for something you dislike.

There are many excellent books that you'll want to share with the children but either won't have time for or won't find appropriate to read aloud to a group, so do a book talk. Tell the children enough about the book to make them want to share it with someone at home. Books that fall into this category include:

- Small format books.
- Books with illustrations that are small or pale.
- Books in which the story is too long. They can be shared in two or more sittings at home.
- Nonfiction titles.
- Wordless books. Children can make up their own words and story at home.
- Books with chapters.
- Books that require a special child to appreciate them.
- Books in which the text is interrupted for several pages by illustrations.
- Books in which text also appears in the illustrations.
- Books that are different editions of stories used as read alouds.

You'll also select other material to use in your programs to provide a change of pace and to offer other experiences with language. Tell-and-draw stories are short tales that evolve on a chalkboard or a piece of paper. Fold-and-cut stories culminate in a paper creation that you cut out as you tell the rhyme, story, or song.

Many titles can be turned into felt-board or flannel-board stories. Look for stories that do not require a lot of characters, settings, or objects. You don't want to manipulate too many items. Stories that work well on the felt board include *Moon Bear* by Frank Asch, *Why the Sun and the Moon Live in the Sky* by Dayrell Elphinstone, *Caps for Sale* by Esphyr Slobodkina, and *Hattie and the Fox* by Mem Fox. Some rhymes and songs can be turned into felt-board stories too. Don't forget poems. Many lend themselves to interpretation on the felt board.

Choose poems that are within the children's ability to understand, with appropriate language and images. Use collections or single poems with illustrations you can show to a group. Examine poetry books written by Jack Prelutsky and those edited by Lenore Blegvad. Don't forget Mother Goose because children like to hear poems that are familiar to them. Check out Mother Goose collections illustrated by Marguerite de Angeli, Tomie dePaola, and Brian Wildsmith. Children also like stories in verse, such as *May I Bring a Friend?* by Beatrice Schenk de Regniers.

Most participation books for this age group are visual guessing games. Many clever titles are available including Tana Hoban's *Look Again* and *Puzzles* by Brian Wildsmith.

Children enjoy fingerplays with broad and easy actions. Counting hand rhymes are popular, and you'll find a generous selection of them. Action rhymes are also particularly successful. Children have the opportunity to move their entire bodies, not just their hands or fingers.

Children like to sing, and there are many popular tunes and folk songs you can share with them. Use songs with repetition, such as "Old MacDonald Had a Farm" and "This Old Man." Children either know the song or quickly catch on to the tune and the words. Beautifully illustrated versions of individual songs exist, and they are perfect to share with a group. Don't forget to use action songs such as "I'm a Little Teapot," in which the children sing and do simple actions. Check out the wonderful records and collections of songs by Raffi. Children and adults are delighted by Raffi and his music.

Creative dramatics work well in programs too. Select rhymes, poems, short stories, or parts of stories that children can act out.

Most filmstrips for children are based on picture-book stories and use the text and illustrations from the books. They vary considerably in quality, so use them selectively. Use a filmstrip version of a book when:

- The book is too small for group presentation.

- The sound track enhances the story.

- The narrator (sometimes the author of the book) gives an excellent interpretation of the story.

- There are a few textless pages in the book that can be bridged with music in the filmstrip.

Some excellent films have been produced for children. And, while many children have seen the films because of the easy accessibility of cable television, they like to see them again. Use the same criteria you would use in evaluating books to select appropriate films.

It's worth keeping track of material that you find on eight-by-five-inch file cards or in a notebook. List the program subject, and then leave ample space to enter titles for each heading: read alouds, book talks, other story forms, poetry, fingerplays and action rhymes, songs, films and filmstrips, and activities.

ORGANIZING AND ARRANGING THE MATERIAL

A program thirty to forty-five minutes long works well with four and five year olds. Be flexible, though. If the children are restless for a particular session (it's a rainy day; it's Halloween), don't use all of your material.

There are several ways to open your program. You might:

- Have a short discussion on the topic.
- Tell a one- or two-minute story.
- Do a book talk.
- Share a poem.
- Settle everyone down with a fingerplay.

Place longer stories at the beginning of the program when everyone is most attentive. Use fingerplays, action rhymes, or songs as a change of pace within the program. Participation books, creative dramatics, and other activities are best shared at the end of the program. It's often difficult for children to settle down after these. Films and filmstrips work well near the end of the program, but like shorter stories, other story forms, book talks, and poetry, they can be used in whatever slot seems appropriate.

PREPARING FOR THE STORY HOUR

Don't rely on an off-the-cuff performance. Be familiar with your material. Practice the stories you intend to read aloud, and think of short comments to introduce each story.

Extemporaneous book talks are effective. Write your talk on a file card, in note form preferably, and use the card as a reference. Don't recite the entire plot. Instead, set up the dilemma, problem, or conflict in the book. Reveal enough to entice someone to bring the book home and find out "what happened next." Mark illustrations from the book that correspond to your comments. Share these illustrations when you do the book talk.

Practice fingerplays and action rhymes until you can do them easily without the book. Practice felt-board stories until you can manipulate the felt pieces smoothly. The same adage applies to tell-and-draw stories and fold-and-cut stories.

You can buy a felt board or you can make one. Take a piece of wood about twenty-four by thirty inches, stretch a piece of felt over it, and then tack the felt to the board with heavy staples. Story pieces are best made out of felt.

"Preview" is the key word when using filmstrips and films. You don't want any surprises during the program. Be sure that the film or filmstrip you purchased or borrowed is the correct title. Also, check that a borrowed film does not run backward, upside down, or jumpy. Be sure that the sound is audible. If you borrow a film or filmstrip and find that the colors are flat, the pacing is too slow, or it's inappropriate for four and five year olds, don't use it.

While preparing for the story hour, jot down comments that will connect each book or activity to the next item or to other items in the program. These comments lend coherence to your material.

AGE OF CHILDREN

You'll find that you can share a greater variety of stories and activities with four and five year olds than you can with three to five year olds. If possible, hold a separate program for three year olds.

THE SERIES

A series is effective because it takes children and their parents time to get used to coming to story hour. A series of programs also gives you the chance to develop a rapport with the children. And, you can develop programs ranging from those which use simple materials to those which use longer, more complex stories and activities.

You can run your program from fall through spring, in ten-week sessions, or in six-week sessions—the length of the series depends on interest, your schedule, and staffing. Some programmers break during the winter months when attendance falls off due to sickness or bad weather. Other programmers begin in October because they need September to plan programs after a hectic summer schedule.

REGISTRATION

It's advisable to hold a registration period for the entire series. The registration allows you to limit the size of your group. Twenty to twenty-five preschoolers is usually the most one person can handle and still do an effective program. Take additional names on a waiting list in case anyone drops out. If demand is great, you might need two story-hour sessions. You can hold the registration for several days, a week, or until the maximum number of children has signed up.

Some programmers let people register over the phone. However, there are advantages to registering children in person: you can meet the children, and they can meet you; you can familiarize the children with the library if they haven't visited before; and you can answer the parents' or the care givers' questions. You'll have the opportunity to explain the format and the purpose of the program to the adults and orient them to library services. Also, you can take special considerations into account before the series begins. If a child has a hearing or visual impairment, he or she can be seated at the front of the group.

Give the parent or the care giver a form to fill out. On the bottom of the form, ask for information including child's name, address, phone number, age, and name of parent. The rest of the form, which you give to the adult, lists information about the program. This handout also serves as a reminder about the program.

PUBLICITY

The amount and kind of publicity needed will vary. If the story hour is an established program in your community, then people will probably ask you about it. If attendance hasn't been good in past years or you're initiating story hour in your area, then you'll want to use most or all of the different types of publicity available.

Write an article for the local newspaper's community bulletin board. Be sure to include the name and a brief description of the program, age of registrants, time, day, dates, location, name of contact person, and phone number. Radio stations air announcements for nonprofit institutions. Be concise! Many local cable television stations also air public-service announcements. Contact the station for details on how it wants the information to be submitted.

If you film story hours, use some of your footage to create an ad for the cable television station's community-access channel. If you're lucky, the station will provide a volunteer to help you with your idea. Here's a storyboard for an ad:

Audio	Video
Would you like your preschooler to enjoy good books?	Children listening to story
Would you like your preschooler to enjoy fingerplays, rhymes, songs, and filmstrips?	Children doing fingerplay
Would you like your child to catch the reading habit?	Children listening to story
Then put your child in the picture.	Group of children
Sign up for picture book story hour.	Group of children
(Audio same as video)	For more information, call the Thomas Crane Public Library, 471-2400

Posters can be effective especially if they have striking visuals. You might use an illustration or a photograph of children's faces with the slogan "Put Your Child in the Picture, Sign Up for Picture Book Story Hour." Include program information. Tack posters in the children's room; the adult department of the library where parents will see them; and local stores where adults and children go, i.e., grocery, shoe, and clothing stores.

Bookmarks, handouts, and flyers with program information on them can be effective too. Cut bookmarks out in interesting shapes, such as a bookworm or a rocket ship. Use interesting visuals on your handouts and flyers—a carousel or a character from a book that you'll be sharing during the story hour. Don't just leave these items on a desk or table. Hand them to people. Mail flyers to local parents' cooperatives.

LOCATION AND SPACE REQUIREMENTS

A separate program room has many advantages. It can be set up at all times for programming, and during the program, there won't be interruptions from other library activities. If the room is very large, define a smaller area for the program so the children won't move all around. I solved this problem by placing my seat near a wall and putting a table of display books behind the children.

If a separate room is not available, try to find a quiet corner of the children's area. Define the program space with a rug or rug squares on which the children can sit.

Be sure the children don't face anything distracting such as a window or a corridor. A bookcase serves as a good neutral backdrop.

Often you don't have a choice about the amount of space available to you. However, if you do, try to use an area at least twelve feet square.

YOU'RE ON—THE PROGRAM

Here are a few suggestions to consider:

Make name tags for each child. Keep them simple—a ball, a bear, a top. The tags can be attached with a safety pin or strung with a piece of yarn. Name tags are especially helpful when you're trying to learn each child's name.

If you can, sit on a low bench. A bench places you closer to the children than a chair, and it's less formal. Whether the children sit on a rug, rug squares, or cushions, try to arrange them in a semicircle so they can all see you and the books clearly.

Before the program begins, ask the parents and the care givers to leave the program space. You should emphasize this at the registration. Children often behave differently in front of their parents. Sometimes, the adults are noisy, and you compete with them for the children's attention. Perhaps there's a room they can go to if they have younger children with them. If this isn't possible, ask them to sit away from the program space.

Preface each book with the title and the name of the author and illustrator. Hold each read aloud in one hand slightly away from and in front of your body. Panning or moving the book from side to side isn't necessary and it can be distracting.

In general, it's best to let the story speak for itself. Interjections can be annoying. If you ask questions about a story, be sure that you can relate the children's comments to the next activity.

When you do a book talk, show illustrations from the book that correspond to what you're talking about. When you share a filmstrip or film, try to have a copy of the accompanying book if one exists or is available.

Never force the children to participate in an activity. Let them watch and join at their own pace.

Discipline problems can occur even if you have excellent material and a lively presentation. Don't ignore these incidents. Address the problem immediately and firmly. If a child is talking, interject the child's name into the story. An example is " 'Timmy' the little red hen said...." Sometimes one child annoys another. Separate them and seat one of them near you. Don't let anyone spoil the group's good time.

PROGRAMS FOR PARENTS

A logical companion to the story hour is programs for the parents and care givers. Ask a librarian from the adult department to give a talk on child-care books, how-to-books, cookbooks, financial management books, or any other subject you think would interest these adults.

Invite a school psychologist to talk about preparing children for the first day of school. Ask the supervisor of children's services to talk about books to use with children of various ages.

EVALUATION

It's worth taking a few minutes after each story hour to note how successful each book or activity was and if each item's placement in the program was effective. These steps will help you plan future programs.

Balloons:
Large and Small

PUBLICITY

Decorate your bulletin board with toy balloons or hot-air balloons made out of construction paper. You might prefer to create a hot-air balloon scene with balloons soaring over fields or show children in a park buying toy balloons from a vendor. Handouts with either type of balloon drawn on them are easy to do. Make a poster in the shape of a hot-air balloon and include program information on the basket.

PROGRAM PLAN

Hang toy balloons in the program area. Perhaps you have a balloon towel, model, or ornament to add to your space.

Introduction

Introduce the program: "Balloons come in all sizes, large and small. There are hot-air balloons that take you soaring into the sky or toy balloons you can hold in your hand. Did you know that balloons can lead people into adventures or can have adventures all by themselves? They do in the stories we'll share today."

Read Aloud

The Great Town & Country Bicycle Balloon Chase by Barbara Douglass. il. by
   Carol Newsom. New York: Lothrop, Lee & Shepard Books, 1984.
   Introduce the story: "Gina and Grandpa are going to take part in the balloon chase. People will ride their bicycles to try to be first to touch the hot-air balloon when it lands. Grandpa and Gina know it won't be easy because no one can tell where the balloon will go."

Book Talk

The Balloon Trip by Ron Wegen. il. by author. New York: Clarion Books,
   1981.
   Introduce the story: "Here's a different look at a hot-air balloon — from inside the balloon. Join a boy, a girl, and their father as they float in a balloon through the sky. They see many interesting sights including the Statue of Liberty. They even touch the treetops. It's a fun trip, but it turns scary when a storm threatens them."

Action Rhyme

"Balloon Adventure" by Paula Gaj Sitarz.
   Introduce the rhyme: "In our first story we joined Gina and Grandpa as they chased a hot-air balloon. In *The Balloon Trip* we saw what everything looks like from inside the balloon. Now let's pretend to be a hot-air balloon."
   There are several broad movements in this rhyme. Be sure you have a large space in which the children can move. Demonstrate the rhyme for the youngsters. Then invite them to join you and repeat.

Balloon Adventure

The balloon lies flat on the ground.
(Lie flat on floor.)

A fan and flame blow hot air round.
(Pretend to blow air.)

The balloon gets bigger and soon stands so high.
(Slowly stand and puff out arms.)

It lifts over houses and into sky.
(Stand on toes.)

It floats along with the wind and breeze.
(Sway body.)

It lifts and dips and grazes the trees.
(Squat down. Brush air with fingertips.)

And as the balloon touches gently down,
(Float slowly to floor.)

It loses air and soon melts to the ground.
(Lie flat on floor.)

Read Aloud

The Big Yellow Balloon by Edward Fenton. il. by Ib Ohlsson. Garden City, N.Y.: Doubleday, 1967.

Introduce the story: "Just because a toy balloon is smaller than a hot-air balloon doesn't mean you have less fun or less excitement with them. Roger finds that out. One day he goes for a walk with the big yellow balloon he bought. Someone is very interested in Roger's balloon. Before you know it Roger is followed by many people and animals. He's in the middle of an adventure all because of this balloon, and he doesn't even know it."

Fingerplay

"Balloons," p. 79 in *Ring a Ring O'Roses: Stories, Games and Finger Plays for Pre-School Children*, rev. ed. Flint, Mich.: Flint Public Library, 1981.

Introduce the fingerplay: "Let's blow up a toy balloon and then pop it. It will be noisy, so block your ears."

This fingerplay is easy to do. Invite the children to imitate your actions. They'll probably want to repeat this quick rhyme several times.

Balloons

This is the way we blow
    our balloons,
Blow, blow, blow.

(Pretend to blow, rounding hands as if holding a balloon, spreading further and further apart.)

This is the way we break
    our balloons,
Oh! Oh! Oh!

(Clap hands together on each "Oh!")

Fingerplay

"Little Balloon," p. 82 in *Ring a Ring O' Roses: Stories, Games and Finger
    Plays for Pre-School Children*, rev. ed. Flint, Mich.: Flint Public Library,
    1981.
   Introduce the fingerplay: "Sometimes toy balloons break by accident,
without you trying to pop them. That's what happens to the young person in
this short story."
   There are several easy motions in this rhyme which you can demonstrate
for the children. Then invite them to join you and repeat.

Little Balloon

I had a little balloon	(Make circle with hands.
That I hugged tight to me.	(Hug self tight.)
There was a great big BANG!	(Clap hands loudly.)
No more balloon, you see.	
But if I had this many more,	(Hold up five fingers.)
I wouldn't hug them tight!	(Shake head 'no.')
I'd just hold onto the strings	(Grasp strings.)
And fly up like a kite.	(Raise both arms high.)

Read Aloud

A Balloon for Grandad by Nigel Gray. il. by Jane Ray. New York: Orchard
    Books, 1988.
   Introduce the story: "Sam is sad. The wind took his red and silver balloon
and sent it up into the sky. But Sam's dad knows how to make Sam feel better.
Sam's dad might be able to make Sam feel happy about his lost balloon."

Book Talk

I Don't Care by Marjorie Weinman Sharmat. il. by Lillian Hoban. New York:
    Macmillan, 1977.
   Introduce the story: "Like Sam, Jonathan has a toy balloon. It's blue with
a smiling face. Jonathan likes his balloon. He enjoys watching it go up and
down. What would Jonathan do if something happened to his balloon?"

Activities

"Fizzle Fun," p. 69 in *I Saw a Purple Cow: and 100 Other Recipes for Learning*
    by Ann Cole, Carolyn Haas, Faith Bushnell, and Betty Weinberger. il. by
    True Kelley. Boston: Little, Brown, 1972.
   Introduce the activity: "We've shared several stories about toy balloons
today. Have you ever tried to blow up a balloon? It's not easy to do, is it? I can
show you a simple way to blow up a balloon without putting it to your mouth
and blowing air into it."

You'll be demonstrating how a deflated balloon inflates when it's placed over the neck of a bottle in which you've put baking soda and vinegar. Have several bottles and balloons at your table. The children will want to see this several times.

TRY THIS!

Read Aloud

Calhoun, Mary. *Hot-Air Henry*. il. by Erick Ingraham. New York: William Morrow, 1981.

Wildsmith, Brian. *Bear's Adventure*. il. by author. New York: Pantheon, 1982.

Book Talk

Adams, Adrienne. *The Great Valentine's Day Balloon Race*. il. by author. New York: Scribner's, 1980.

Carrick, Carol, and Donald Carrick. *The Highest Balloon on the Common*. il. by Donald Carrick. New York: Greenwillow, 1977.

Hughes, Shirley. *Up and Up*. il. by author. Englewood Cliffs, N.J.: Prentice-Hall, 1979. (This is a wordless book.)

Mari, Iela. *The Magic Balloon*. il. by author. New York: S. G. Phillips, 1967. (This is a wordless book.)

Poetry

"The Balloon," p. 111 by Karla Kuskin in *Pocket Full of Posies* compiled and written by Gertrude Keyworth. il. by Jerry Ryle and Lorraine Conaway. Flint, Mich.: Flint Public Library, 1984.

"The Balloon Man," p. 76 by Dorothy Aldis in *Tomie dePaola's Book of Poems*. il. by Tomie dePaola. New York: Putnam, 1988.

Fingerplay and Action Rhyme

"My Balloon," p. 4 in *Kidstuff*, vol. 2, no. 5, "Toys and Play" edited by Sheila Debs. Lake Park, Fla.: GuideLines Press, 1983.

"My Circus Balloon," p. 4 in *Kidstuff*, vol. 1, no. 2, "Razzle Dazzle Circus" edited by Sheila Debs. Lake Park, Fla.: GuideLines Press, 1981.

"My Red Balloon," in *My Big Book of Fingerplays: A Fun-to-Say, Fun-to-Play Collection* by Daphne Hogstrom. il. by Sally Augustiny. Racine, Wis.: Western Publishing, 1974. unpaged.

Splish! Splash!
It's Bathtime

PUBLICITY

Handouts and posters cut in the shape of a bar of soap, a towel, or a bathtub are eyecatching. Make a poster using a real bath towel by attaching a stiff piece of paper, which includes program information, to the center of the towel. Decorate your bulletin board with items associated with taking a bath. Add a child in a bathtub to the center of your picture or simply cover your board with soap bubbles made out of construction paper. Soap bubbles can be drawn on handouts and posters too.

PROGRAM PLAN

Decorate the program area with articles used at bathtime. Drape a robe or a towel over your chair and hang a soap on a rope nearby. You might like to wear a shower cap and a bathrobe during story hour. Invite the children to sit on bath towels.

Introduction

Talk to the children about bathtime. You can direct the discussion with questions like, "Who likes to take a bath? Why do you like to take a bath? What do you say so you won't have to get out of the tub? Who doesn't like to hop in the tub? Why? What excuses do you give not to take a bath?"

Book Talk

I Hate to Take a Bath by Judi Barrett. il. by Charles B. Slackman. New York: Four Winds Press, 1975.
Introduce the story: "We know what we like and don't like about bathtime. If you share this book with someone at home you'll find out what another group of children enjoys or doesn't enjoy about baths. Maybe you share some of their feelings about goose bumps, getting ears washed, bubble baths, splashing, and fingers that look like raisins."

Read Aloud

No Bath Tonight by Jane Yolen. il. by Nancy Winslow Parker. New York: Thomas Y. Crowell, 1978.
Introduce the story: "Let's meet a young boy who doesn't want to take a bath. Everyday he has a very good reason why he can't — he's hurt his foot, he's hurt his nose. Can anyone convince him that he should take a bath?"

Read Aloud

Harry the Dirty Dog by Gene Zion. il. by Margaret Bloy Graham. New York: Harper & Row, 1956.
Introduce the story: "Harry the dog is like some people including the boy we just met. Harry hates baths. He has his own plan for not taking a bath. Let's see if it works."

Book Talk

To Bathe a Boa by Charlene Imbior Kudrna. il. by author. Minneapolis, Minn.: Carolrhoda Books, 1986.

Introduce the story: "It isn't only dogs who don't like baths. Boa constrictors don't like them either according to this story. If you had a pet boa how would you get it to take a bath? Could you trick him into it? What if you tried to force it? Share this book with an adult and see what happens when a young boy tries to make his pet snake take a bath."

Poetry

"Before the Bath," p. 26 by Corinna Marsh in *Read-Aloud Rhymes for the Very Young*, selected by Jack Prelutsky. il. by Marc Brown. New York: Alfred A. Knopf, 1986.

Introduce the poem: "The child in this poem worries about how cold it is before he hops in the tub. But what's it like *in* the tub?"

Action Rhyme

"After a Bath," p. 39 in *Ring a Ring O' Roses: Stories, Games and Finger Plays for Pre-School Children*, rev. ed. Flint, Mich.: Flint Public Library, 1981.

Introduce the action rhyme: "Once you've taken a bath does it take you a long time to dry off? Here's a suggestion for making it easier."

This action rhyme can be done seated or standing. Try it with the children at least twice.

After a Bath

After my bath, I try, try, try	(Suit action to words.)

After my bath, I try, try, try   (Suit action to words.)
To wipe myself 'till I'm dry, dry, dry.
Hands to wipe, and fingers and toes,
And two wet legs and a shiny nose.
Just think, how much less time I'd take,
If I were a dog, and could shake, shake, shake.

Read Aloud

Andrew's Bath by David McPhail. il. by author. Boston: Little, Brown, 1984.

Introduce the story: "Unlike Harry the dog and the boy we met in the first story I shared, Andrew doesn't mind taking a bath. He thinks that he can give himself a better bath than his parents give him. Can he?"

Book Talk

The Bathtub Ocean by Diane Paterson. il. by author. New York: Dial Press, 1979.

Introduce the story: "Andrew had an exciting time in the tub. Henry's tub is a fascinating place too. There's a whale to ride, sailfish to sail, a starfish, an octopus, and more. It's an ocean full of adventures."

Read Aloud

Five Minute's Peace by Jill Murphy. il. by author. New York: Putnam, 1986.
　　Introduce the story: "Mother Elephant wants some quiet time so she's going to soak in the bathtub. But will her bath be relaxing? Will the children leave mother alone?"

Action Rhyme

"Andrew's Bath" by Paula Gaj Sitarz.
　　Introduce the rhyme: "Like Andrew in the story, the Andrew in this rhyme enjoys taking his bath."
　　Demonstrate the actions in this rhyme for the children and then invite them to join you. Repeat at least once.

Andrew's Bath

Andrew, Andrew hop in the tub.
(Hop and sit down.)

Andrew, Andrew scrub, scrub, scrub.
(Scrub body.)

Andrew, Andrew clean your toes.
(Rub toes.)

Andrew, Andrew wash your nose.
(Dab nose.)

Andrew, Andrew float your tug.
(Make wavy motion with right hand.)

Andrew, Andrew hop on the rug.
(Hop and stand.)

Andrew, Andrew dry off so.
(Shake back and forth.)

Andrew, Andrew to bed we go.
(Sit down and rest head on hands.)

Activities

"Bathtime Memory Game" developed by Paula Gaj Sitarz.
　　Before the program: Assemble items used in the bath. These might include: a bottle of shampoo, bar of soap, sponge, face cloth, toy boat, faucet cover, rubber duck, and a scrub brush. Put a few of the articles on a tray.
　　During the program: Give the children a minute to look at the articles on the tray. Cover the tray and let the children recall what they saw. Try this game a few times as long as the children remain interested. Change the items and the number of items each time.

TRY THIS!

Read Aloud

Allen, Pamela. *Mr. Archimedes' Bath.* il. by author. N.Y.: Lothrop, Lee & Shepard Books, 1980.

Cole, Brock. *No More Baths.* il. by author. Garden City, N.Y.: Doubleday, 1980.

Gantos, Jack. *Swampy the Alligator.* il. by Nicole Rubel. New York: Windmill Books and Wanderer Books, 1980.

Wood, Audrey. *King Bidgood's in the Bathtub.* il. by Don Wood. New York: Harcourt Brace Jovanovich, 1985.

Book Talk

Burningham, John. *Time to Get Out of the Bath, Shirley.* il. by author. New York: Thomas Y. Crowell, 1978.

Buxbaum, Susan Kovaes and Rita Golden Gelman. *Splash! All About Baths.* il. by Maryann Cocca-Leffler. Boston: Little, Brown, 1987.

Henkes, Kevin. *Clean Enough.* il. by author. New York: Greenwillow, 1982.

Kunhardt, Edith. *Where's Peter?* il. by author. New York: Greenwillow, 1988.

Paterson, Diane. *Soap and Suds.* il. by author. New York: Alfred A. Knopf, 1984

Poetry

"After a Bath," p. 42 by Aileen Fisher in *The Read-Aloud Treasury* compiled by Joanna Cole and Stephanie Calmenson. il. by Ann Schweninger. Garden City, N.Y.: Doubleday, 1988.

"Naughty Soap Song," p. 26 by Dorothy Aldis; "Happy Winter, Steamy Tub" by Karen Gundersheimer and "The Way They Scrub," by A. B. Ross, p. 27 in *Read-Aloud Rhymes for the Very Young* selected by Jack Prelutsky. il. by Marc Brown. New York: Alfred A. Knopf, 1986.

Fingerplay and Action Rhyme

"Bath Time," p. 5 and "Washing Myself," p. 6 in *Finger Frolics: Over 250 Fingerplays for Young Children from 3 Years*, rev. ed. compiled by Liz Cromwell, Dixie Hibner, and John R. Faitel. il. by Joan Lockwood. Livonia, Mich.: Partner Press, 1983.

"Hands and Face" by Paula Gaj Sitarz.

Hands and Face

I turn on the faucet.   (Suit actions to words.)
I grab the soap
Oops, it slips from my hands!
I start again and wash my face,
My ears,
My nose just so.
And then my hands I scrub and scrub.
Whew! I'm glad that's done.

Goodnight, Sleep Tight:
Bedtime Stories

Do this program as a regular story hour or as a bedtime story hour. If you do the latter invite the children to wear pajamas and to bring their favorite stuffed animal.

PUBLICITY

Decorate your bulletin board simply with a quilt fashioned out of felt or construction paper. Create another easy board display with pillows made of felt or cloth. Perhaps you'd rather depict a child holding a blanket, children having a pillow fight, or a child's face with eyes closed. You might design a nighttime scene of a child in bed near a window through which the moon and the stars shine. Cut out handouts and posters in the shape of a pillow, a blanket, or a pair of pajamas.

PROGRAM PLAN

Set a bedroom lamp on a table near you and a few pillows as well. If you feel particularly strong, bring in a rocking chair to sit in while you read stories or sit on a quilt. Wear a nightcap, a nightshirt, a robe, and/or slippers. Have the children sit on a blanket, bedspread, or quilt.

Introduction

Introduce the program: "Do you like to go to bed at night? Do you like to snuggle under the covers? Or do you take your time going to bed and give excuses so you won't have to? We're going to share stories in which some children like to go to sleep and others don't."

Poetry

"Night Comes," p. 65 by Beatrice Schenk de Regniers, "Bedtime," p. 66 by Eleanor Farjeon, and "Sleeping Outdoors," p. 65 by Marchette Chute in *Read-Aloud Rhymes for the Very Young* selected by Jack Prelutsky. il. by Marc Brown. New York: Alfred A. Knopf, 1986.
Introduce the first two poems: "Let's hear two different children's thoughts about the night and bedtime."
Show the accompanying illustrations from the book to the children as you share "Night Comes" and "Bedtime" with them.
Introduce the last poem: "Here's a short poem that you can learn with me."
"Sleeping Outdoors" is a short poem which lends itself to telling on the felt board. You will need the following items made of felt: a star, two trees, a blanket, and a young person. Use the illustration in the book as a guide to making your felt pieces.
Recite the poem then read it again and invite the children to repeat each line after you.

Read Aloud

May We Sleep Here Tonight? by Tan Koide. il. by Yasuko Koide. New York: Margaret K. McElderry Book/Atheneum, 1983.

Introduce the story: "It's so foggy! And the house in the woods looks like an inviting place to sleep for many of the animals who get lost while hiking. But who owns the house? Will he or she be angry at the sleepers?"

Fingerplay

"Going to Bed," p. 46 in *Ring a Ring O' Roses: Stories, Games and Finger Plays for Pre-School Children*, rev. ed. Flint, Mich.: Flint Public Library, 1981.

Introduce the fingerplay: "Let's meet a little boy who enjoys going to bed. He knows that once he's had a good night's sleep he'll feel good and ready to play."

There are several actions that require fine motor skills so demonstrate this slowly for the children and then repeat it twice.

Going to Bed

This little boy is just going
   to bed.
Down on the pillow he lays
   his head.
He wraps himself in the covers
   tight.
And this is the way he sleeps all
   night.
Morning comes, he opens his
   eyes.
Off with a toss the covers fly.
Soon he is up and dressed and
   away.
Ready for fun and play all day.

(Use forefinger for boy. Lay finger cross-wise on other hand using thumb for pillow. Use fingers for cover.)

Read Aloud

Henry and the Dragon by Eileen Christelow. il. by author. New York: Clarion Books, 1984.

Introduce the story: "After hearing his father tell him a story about a fierce dragon, Henry Rabbit is convinced that a dragon lives near his house. When Henry goes to bed the shadow on his bedroom wall looks like a dragon. His parents say there is no such thing as a dragon, but Henry thinks there is and he wants to catch it."

Book Talk

Clyde Monster by Robert L. Crowe. il. by Kay Chorao. New York: E. P. Dutton, 1976.

Introduce the story: "Clyde is a friendly little monster who breathes fire in the lake to make steam rise and claws holes in the ground. But at night when it's time to sleep in his cave, Clyde doesn't want to. He's afraid of the dark. What could a monster be afraid of?"

Song

"Hush, Little Baby," p. 12 in *Singing Bee! A Collection of Favorite Children's Songs* compiled by Jane Hart. il. by Anita Lobel. New York: Lothrop, Lee & Shepard Books, 1982.

Introduce the song: "Do you sing songs before you go to bed? Do you remember someone singing to you when you were a baby? This is a song you might have heard or sung before. You might like to share it sometime with a younger brother, sister, or cousin."

Because some of the children probably know this song, sing it through with the group. The song isn't that long so if the children seem interested, repeat.

Read Aloud

Poppy the Panda by Dick Gackenbach. il. by author. New York: Clarion Books, 1984.

Introduce the story: "What will Katie do? Her toy panda, Poppy, refuses to go to bed until he has something nice to wear. Does Katie have anything for Poppy to wear that he will like?"

Read Aloud

Peace at Last by Jill Murphy. il. by author. New York: Dial Press, 1980.

Introduce the story: "Poor Daddy Bear! Mama Bear and Baby Bear are sleeping but he can't get to sleep. It's too noisy. Where can Daddy Bear go to get some quiet and some sleep?"

Poetry

"When All the World's Asleep," p. 64 by Anita E. Posey in *Read-Aloud Rhymes for the Very Young* selected by Jack Prelutsky. il. by Marc Brown. New York: Alfred A. Knopf, 1986.

Introduce the poem: "Do you ever think about where different animals sleep at night? We sleep in beds, but where do turtles, rabbits, and cows sleep?"

Book Talk

If you'd like to know more about where and how animals sleep here are some books for you to look at.

When I'm Sleepy by Jane R. Howard. il. by Lynne Cherry. New York: E. P. Dutton, 1985.

Introduce the story: "Join the little girl in this book as she thinks about what it would be like to sleep somewhere other than in her own bed. What would it be like to sleep in a swamp with an alligator or on a mountain ledge with a goat?"

Good Night to Annie by Eve Merriam. il. by John Wallner. New York: Four Winds Press, 1980.

Introduce the story: "Join Annie. For each letter of the alphabet she sees an animal whose name begins with that letter and who is getting ready to sleep or is asleep."

The Sleepy Book by Charlotte Zolotow. il. by Ilse Plume. New York: Harper & Row Junior Books, 1988.
Introduce the story: "Do you know where moths sleep? Or cranes? Where do spiders, caterpillars, and horses sleep? How do these animals sleep? If you're interested share this book with someone at home."

Activities

"Animal-Sleeping Guessing Game" developed by Paula Gaj Sitarz.
Before the program: Cut out different animals and their sleeping places from illustrations found in magazines, or photocopy pictures of animals and their sleeping places from books. Back the illustrations with felt. You can also make the animals and their sleeping places out of felt.
During the program: Place a row of sleeping places and a row of animals on the board. Ask the children to match each animal to its correct sleeping place.
You can use the book-talk books from above for ideas for this game. Here are some suggestions:

    turtles — shell
    robin — nest
    rabbits, foxes — holes
    bears — cave
    lion — den
    cow — barn
    pig — pen
    horse — barn
    dog — doghouse
    cat — basket
    parakeet — cage
    baby — crib
    child — bed

TRY THIS!

Read Aloud

Arnold, Tedd. *No Jumping on the Bed!* il. by author. New York: Dial Books for Young Readers, 1987.

Brown, Margaret Wise. *Goodnight Moon.* il. by Clement Hurd. New York: Harper & Row, 1947.

Field, Eugene. *Wynken, Blynken & Nod.* il. by Susan Jeffers. New York: E. P. Dutton, 1982.

Hurd, Thatcher. *The Quiet Evening.* il. by author. New York: Greenwillow, 1978.

Keats, Ezra Jack. *Dreams*. il. by author. New York: Macmillan, 1974.

Keller, Holly. *Ten Sleepy Sheep*. il. by author. New York: Greenwillow, 1983.

Levine, Joan. *Bedtime Story*. il. by Gail Owens. New York: E. P. Dutton, 1975.

Loh, Morag. *Tucking Mommy In*. il. by Donna Rawlins. New York: Orchard Books, 1987.

Oppenheim, Joanne. *The Story Book Prince*. il. by Rosanne Litzinger. San Diego, Calif.: Gulliver Books/Harcourt Brace Jovanovich, 1987.

Paxton, Tom. *Jennifer's Rabbit*. il. by Donna Ayers. New York: Morrow Junior Books, 1988.

Plath, Sylvia. *The Bed Book*. il. by Emily McCully. New York: Harper & Row, 1976.

Russo, Marisabina. *Why Do Grown-Ups Have All the Fun?* il. by author. New York: Greenwillow, 1987.

Schertle, Alice. *Goodnight, Hattie, My Dearie, My Dove*. il. by Linda Strauss Edwards. New York: Lothrop, Lee & Shepard Books, 1985.

Sendak, Maurice. *In the Night Kitchen*. il. by author. New York: Harper & Row, 1970.

Stevenson, James. *Bedtime for Bear*. il. by Lynn Munsinger. Boston: Houghton Mifflin, 1985.

10 Bears in My Bed: A Goodnight Countdown. il. by Stanley Mack. New York: Pantheon Books, 1974. (This adapts well as a felt-board story or a creative dramatics activity.)

Ten in a Bed. il. by Mary Rees. Boston: Joy Street/Little, Brown, 1988.

Waber, Bernard. *Ira Sleeps Over*. il. by author. Boston: Houghton Mifflin, 1972.

Wood, Audrey. *The Napping House*. il. by Don Wood. New York: Harcourt Brace Jovanovitch, 1984.

Zeifert, Harriet. *I Won't Go to Bed!* il. by Andrea Baruffi. Boston: Little, Brown, 1987.

Zemach, Margot. *Hush Little Baby*. il. by author. New York: E. P. Dutton, 1976.

Book Talk

Asch, Frank. *Goodnight Horsey*. il. by author. Englewood Cliffs, N.J.: Prentice-Hall, 1981.

Barrett, Judi. *I Hate to Go to Bed*. il. by Ray Cruz. New York: Four Winds Press, 1977.

Chorao, Kay. *Lemon Moon*. il. by author. New York: Holiday House, 1983.

Dragonwagon, Crescent. *Half a Moon and One Whole Star*. il. by Jerry Pinkney. New York: Macmillan, 1986.

Hazen, Barbara Shook. *The Gorilla Did It*. il. by Ray Cruz. New York: Atheneum, 1974.

Hughes, Shirley. *Bedtime at Alfie's*. il. by author. New York: Lothrop, Lee & Shepard Books, 1984.

Jonas, Ann. *The Quilt*. il. by author. New York: Greenwillow, 1984.

Khalsa, Dayal Kaur. *Sleepers*. il. by author. New York: Clarkson N. Potter, 1988.

Kitamura, Satoshi. *When Sheep Cannot Sleep, The Counting Book*. New York: Farrar, Straus and Giroux, 1986.

Ryan, Cheli Durán. *Hilidid's Night*. il. by Arnold Lobel. New York: Macmillan, 1971.

Schmögner, Walter. *The Children's Dream Book*. text by Friedrich C. Heller. translated by Georgess McHargue. il. by Walter Schmogner. Garden City, N.Y.: Doubleday, 1972.

Other Story Forms

"Wee Willie Winkie Runs," p. 308 in *Handbook for Storytellers* by Caroline Feller Bauer. Chicago: American Library Association, 1977. (This is a fold-and-cut story.)

Poetry

"Deedle, Deedle, Dumpling," p. 32 in *The Read-Aloud Treasury* compiled by Joanna Cole and Stephanie Calmenson. il. by Ann Schweninger. Garden City, N.Y.: Doubleday, 1988.

"Diddle, Diddle, Dumpling, My Son John," p. 57 in *Tomie dePaola's Mother Goose*. il. by Tomie dePaola. New York: Putnam, 1985.

Hopkins, Lee Bennett. *Go to Bed! A Book of Bedtime Poems*. il. by Rosekrans Hoffman. New York: Alfred A. Knopf, 1979. (In particular see: "Going to Bed," pp. 6-7 by Marchette Chute; "Bedtime," p. 8 by Eleanor Farjeon; "My Star," p. 11 by Myra Cohn Livingston; and "My Teddy Bear," p. 14 by Margaret Hillert.)

Larrick, Nancy. *When the Dark Comes Dancing: A Bedtime Poetry Book*. il. by John Wallner. New York: Philomel Books, 1983. (In particular see: "Where Do You Sleep?," p. 22 by William Engvik; "All Tucked in & Roasty Toasty," p. 52 by Clyde Watson; and "Hush Little Baby," p. 65.)

Prelutsky, Jack. *My Parents Think I'm Sleeping*. il. by Yossi Abolafia. New York: Greenwillow, 1985. (In particular see: "Rain," pp. 32-33 and "It Is So Still," pp. 34-35.)

Fingerplay and Action Rhyme

"Being Sleepy," p. 7 in *Finger Frolics: Over 250 Fingerplays for Children from 3 Years*, rev. ed. compiled by Liz Cromwell, Dixie Hibner, and John R. Faitel. il. by Joan Lockwood. Livonia, Mich.: Partner Press, 1983.

"Teddy Bear, Teddy Bear," p. 83 in *Ring a Ring O' Roses: Stories, Games and Finger Plays for Pre-School Children*, rev. ed. Flint, Mich.: Flint Public Library, 1981.

"Ten Tired Children," p. 4 and "To Bed, To Bed," p. 5 in *Kidstuff*, vol. 5, no. 2, "It's Time for Bed!" edited by Sheila Debs. Lake Park, Fla.: GuideLines Press, 1988.

"Wee Willie Winkie," in *My Big Book of Fingerplays: A Fun-To-Say, Fun-To-Play Collection* by Daphne Hogstrom. il. by Sally Augustiny. Racine, Wisc.: Western Publishing, 1974. unpaged.

Activities

"I'm Not Sleepy," p. 5 in *Kidstuff*, vol. 5, no. 2, "It's Time for Bed!" edited by Sheila Debs. Lake Park, Fla.: GuideLines Press, 1988. (This is a creative dramatics activity.)

Feathered Friends

PUBLICITY

Cut out photographs of different birds from back issues of magazines and make a collage on your bulletin board. Cover your bulletin board with bird feathers, real or fashioned out of construction paper. Or, you might decorate your bulletin board with bird tracks or bird silhouettes flying through the sky. You could also create a birdhouse with various birds flying near it or place birds on different branches of a large tree. Cut out handouts and posters in the shape of a nest, bird feeder, birdhouse, or birdbath or draw bird tracks on posters and handouts.

PROGRAM PLAN

Do you have a bird feeder or birdhouse that you can hang in the program space? If not, you can make a simple feeder using as a guide: "Birdfeeders," p. 94 in *The Big Book of Recipes for Fun: Creative Learning Activities for Home and School* by Carolyn Buchai Haas. il. by Jane Bennett Phillips. Glencoe, Ill.: cbh Publishing, Inc., 1980. Maybe you've found a bird nest or can borrow one from a children's museum. Use toy stuffed birds to decorate your area.

Introduction

Introduce the program: "There are so many kinds of birds. Some are colorful, others are not. Some birds are small, others large. Birds can be quiet or noisy. There are swimmers and those who don't like the water. There are birds that fly and birds that don't. Birds are as different as people."

Activities

" 'What kind of bird...?' Guessing Game" developed by Paula Gaj Sitarz.

Introduce the activity: "To get us thinking about the different kinds of birds there are, let's play this guessing game. I'll give you clues about a type of bird and you can guess what bird I'm talking about."

You may want to have pictures of all the answers on a board and let the children select their answers from these.

Guessing Game

This bird...
1. Lives in a tree, stays awake at night, blinks a lot, and hoots. (an owl)

2. Lives in places where it is very cold, like the North Pole, walks from side to side, and looks like it's wearing a man's suit or tuxedo.   (a penguin)

3. Lives in the water and has a huge bill which it dips into the water to catch fish and other food.   (a pelican)

4. Can be seen flying around the beach. It is often white, sometimes brown. It swoops into the water, plucks out a clam, soars into the sky, smashes the clam on the rocks, and then eats it.   (a seagull)

5. Has an orange tuft of hair on the top of his head. He likes to peck at trees and makes loud noises with his rat-a-tat-tat. (a woodpecker)

6. Is unlucky. He walks around all year long while the farmer fattens him up for Thanksgiving.   (a turkey)

7. Cannot fly. It has long, long legs and a very long neck. Sometimes it buries its head in the sand.   (an ostrich)

8. Sits on her nest all day long waiting for her eggs to hatch. She clucks a lot, too.   (a hen)

9. Has yellow downy feathers and an orange-colored beak. It loves to swim in the water and it's always quacking. (a duckling)

10. Walks around as if it's very important. It has beautiful, colorful tail feathers.   (a peacock)

Read Aloud

What Kind of Bird Is That? by Mirra Ginsburg. il. by Giulio Maestro. Adapted from a Russian story by V. Suteyev. New York: Crown, 1973.

Introduce the story: "Goose decides to trade necks with a swan but he doesn't stop there. He adds a pelican's beak, the crane's long legs, and, well, let's see what else. Will goose be a more wonderful bird with all these different parts?"

Tell-and-Draw Story

The Wild Ducks and the Goose adapted by Carl Withers. Drawings by Alan E. Cober. New York: Holt, 1968.

Introduce the story: "Meet an old man and his wife who live near a pond. Many wild ducks live on the island in the pond. The old man wants some of those ducks for dinner. Let's see what he plans to do and if his plan works."

Fingerplay

"All Kinds of Birds" by Paula Gaj Sitarz.

Introduce the fingerplay: "We talked about all types of birds during our guessing game. Let's count some birds now. They're doing all sorts of things."

Do this as a counting rhyme. Hold up a finger for each bird. Do this with the children, then repeat.

If you use "All Kinds of Birds" at the end of the program, act it out.

All Kinds of Birds

One pelican dips his bill and catches a fish.   (Hold up one finger for each bird.)

Two peacocks strut and their tail feathers swish.

Three penguins waddle from side to side.

Four owls hoot and blink their eyes.

Five woodpeckers sound rat-a-tat-tats.

Six turkeys gobble and bob like that.

Seven ducks swim and say quack, quack, quack.

Eight chickens cluck and go scratch, scratch, scratch.

Nine ostriches hide their heads in the sand.

Ten seagulls screech as they soar over land.

Birds in the water.   (Make wave motions with arm.)

Birds in the air.   (Flap arms.)

Birds and more birds everywhere!   (Hold arms out wide.)

Read Aloud

Benjy and the Barking Bird by Margaret Bloy Graham. il. by author. New York: Harper & Row, 1971.

Introduce the story: "Benjy the dog does not like it when Aunt Sarah visits because she always brings her parrot, Tilly. Everyone fusses over Tilly and ignores Benjy. Benjy decides that during this visit he'll do something about Tilly for good."

Fingerplay

"Chook, Chook," p. 42 by Anonymous in *Read-Aloud Rhymes for the Very Young* selected by Jack Prelutsky. il. by Marc Brown. New York: Alfred A. Knopf, 1986.

Introduce the fingerplay: "Hens are birds too and here's a story we can share about Mrs. Hen and her children."

Demonstrate this fingerplay. Then do it twice with your group.

"Chook, Chook"
Adapted as fingerplay by Paula Gaj Sitarz.

Chook, chook, chook, chook, chook,
(Bob head and flap arms.)

Good morning, Mrs. Hen.
How many chickens have you got?

Madam, I've got ten.
(Hold up ten fingers.)

Four of them are yellow.
(Hold up four fingers on left hand.)

And four of them are brown,
(Hold up four fingers on right hand.)

And two of them are speckled red,
(Hold up thumbs.)

The nicest in the town.
(Hold arms out wide.)

Read Aloud

Hattie and the Fox by Mem Fox. il. by Patricia Mullins. Scarsdale, N.Y.:
    Bradbury Press, 1986.
    Introduce the story: "Let's meet another hen. Hattie the big black hen sees
and senses danger in the bush. The first thing she spies is a nose peeking out.
Hattie is worried but none of the other animals seem to care. Should they?"

Song

"Bluebird," p. 83 in *Singing Bee! A Collection of Favorite Children's Songs*
    compiled by Jane Hart. il. by Anita Lobel. New York: Lothrop, Lee &
    Shepard Books, 1982.
    Introduce the song: "Besides the birds we've talked about so far there are
many others like sparrows, robins, hummingbirds, and bluebirds. Let's share a
song about a bluebird."
    Sing the first verse for the children so they'll hear the tune. Then repeat
the first verse with the children before going on to the second verse.

Participation Book

But Where is the Green Parrot? by Thomas Zacharias. il. by author. New
    York: Delacorte Press, 1978.
    Introduce the book: "Can you find the parrot in this book? He's hiding on
every page. He might be on a table or in a train."
    Show each double page spread to small sections of the group at a time.
After someone tells you where the parrot is point to the parrot so each child
sees it.

TRY THIS!

Read Aloud

Allen, Jeffrey. *Mary Alice, Operator Number 9*. il. by James Marshall. Boston:
    Little, Brown, 1975.

Duff, Maggie, reteller. *Rum Pum Pum*. il. by Jose Aruego and Ariane Dewey.
    New York: Macmillan, 1978.

Freeman, Don. *Come Again, Pelican*. il. by author. New York: Viking Press, 1961.

Galdone, Paul, reteller. *Henny Penny*. il. by Paul Galdone. New York: The Seabury Press, 1968.

Gay, Michael. *Bibi Takes Flight*. il. by author. New York: William Morrow, 1984.

Kasza, Keiko. *The Wolf's Chicken Stew*. il. by author. New York: Putnam, 1987.

Kraus, Robert. *Owliver*. il. by Jose Aruego and Ariane Dewey. Englewood Cliffs, N.J.: Prentice-Hall Books for Young Readers, 1974.

Lionni, Leo. *Nicholas, Where Have You Been?* il. by author. New York: Alfred A. Knopf, 1987.

The Little Red Hen. il. by Paul Galdone. New York: The Seabury Press, 1973.

Preston, Edna Mitchell. *Squawk to the Moon, Little Goose*. il. by Barbara Cooney. New York: Viking Press, 1974.

Roy, Ronald. *Three Ducks Went Wandering*. il. by Paul Galdone. New York: The Seabury Press, 1979.

Sis, Peter. *Rainbow Rhino*. il. by author. New York: Alfred A. Knopf, 1987.

Stanley, Diane. *Birdsong Lullaby*. il. by author. New York: William Morrow, 1985.

Wildsmith, Brian. *The Owl and the Woodpecker*. il. by author. New York: Franklin Watts: 1972.

Wildsmith, Brian. *Pelican*. il. by author. New York: Pantheon Books, 1982.

Wolkstein, Diane. *The Cool Ride in the Sky*. il. by Paul Galdone. New York: 1973.

Book Talk

Ash, Jutta, reteller. *Wedding Birds*. il. by Jutta Ash. Boston: The Atlantic Monthly Press, 1986.

Carle, Eric. *The Rooster Who Set Out to See the World*. il. by author. New York: Franklin Watts, 1972.

Flack, Marjorie. *The Story about Ping*. il. by Kurt Wiese. New York: Viking Press, 1961.

Thaler, Mike. *Owly*. il. by David Wiesner. New York: Harper & Row, 1982.

Wildsmith, Brian. *Brian Wildsmith's Birds*. il. by author. New York: Oxford University Press, 1980.

Wolff, Ashley. *A Year of Birds*. il. by author. New York: Dodd, Mead, 1984.

Other Story Forms

"Hickety, Pickety My Black Hen," p. 307 in *Handbook for Storytellers* by Caroline Feller Bauer. Chicago, Ill.: American Library Association, 1977.

"Hortense the Chicken," pp. 24-25 in *Tell and Draw Stories* by Margaret J. Olson. Minneapolis, Minn.: Creative Storytime Press, 1963.

Poetry

"Humming Birds," p. 23 by Betty Sage and "Singing in the Spring," p. 23 by Ivy O. Eastwich and "Quack, Quack," p. 43 by Dr. Seuss in *Read-Aloud Rhymes for the Very Young* selected by Jack Prelutsky. il. by Marc Brown. New York: Alfred A. Knopf, 1986.

"To Be a Duck," p. 18 by Aileen Fisher in *Pocket Full of Posies* compiled and written by Gertrude Keyworth. il. by Jerry Ryle and Lorraine Conaway. Flint, Mich.: Flint Public Library, 1984.

Fingerplay and Action Rhyme

"Five Little Chickadees," pp. 27-28 in *One Two Three Four: Number Rhymes and Finger Games* compiled by Mary Grice. il. by Denis Wrigley. New York: Frederick Warne, 1970.

"Five Little Ducks," p. 36; "Little Bird," p. 37; "Sing a Song of Sixpence," p. 55; and "Two Little Blackbirds," p. 73 in *Let's Do Fingerplays* by Marion F. Grayson. il. by Nancy Weyl. Washington, D.C.: Robert B. Luce, 1962.

"Five Little Owls in an Old Elm-Tree." Adapted as fingerplay by Paula Gaj Sitarz from an anonymous poem.

"Five Little Owls in an Old Elm-Tree"

Five little owls in an old elm-tree,
(Hold up five fingers.)

Fluffy and puffy as owls could be,
(Round shoulders and puff out cheeks.)

Blinking and winking with big round eyes.
(Blink eyes.)

At the big round moon that hung in the skies;
(Arms form circle overhead.)

As I passed beneath, I could hear one say,
"There'll be mouse for supper, there will, today."
(Rub stomach.)

Then all of them hooted, "Tu whit, tu whoo!
(Hoot.)

Yes, mouse for supper, Hoo hoo, Hoo hoo!"
(Hoot again.)

"Five Little Robins," "Five Little Squirrels," "Five Old Crows," p. 9 and "If I Were A Bird," p. 11 in *Ring a Ring O' Roses: Stories, Games and Finger Plays for Pre-School Children*, rev. ed. Flint, Mich.: Flint Public Library, 1981.

"Once I Saw a Little Bird." Adapted as fingerplay by Paula Gaj Sitarz from a traditional poem.

"Once I Saw a Little Bird"

Once I saw a little bird,
Come hop, hop, hop,
(Hop right hand in palm of left hand.)

And I cried, "Little bird,
Will you stop, stop, stop?"
(Hold right hand up like a stop sign.)

I was going to the window,
To say "How do you do?"
(Pretend to look out of window.)

But he shook his little tail
And away he flew.
(Flap arms.)

"Ten Little Pigeons," p. 30, "My Pigeon House," and "Two Little Birds," p. 31, "Little Bird," p. 41, and "Wide-Eyed Owl," p. 60 in *Finger Frolics: Over 250 Fingerplays for Children from 3 Years*, rev. ed. compiled by Liz Cromwell, Dixie Hibner, and John R. Faitel. il. by Joan Lockwood. Livonia, Mich.: Partner Press, 1983.

Song

"The Dickey-Bird Song," p. 20 and "Five Little Ducks," p. 26 in *Tom Tinker, Eye Winker, Chin Chopper* by Tom Glazer. il. by Ron Himler. Garden City, N.Y.: Doubleday, 1980.

Film

The Cold-Blooded Penguin. Burbank, Calif.: Walt Disney Company, 1971. 10 min.

Rosie's Walk. Weston, Conn.: Weston Woods, 1971. 4 min.

Six Penguins. Del Mar, Calif.: McGraw-Hill Films, 1971. 5 min.

Under the Big Top:
Circus Stories

PUBLICITY

Create a circus scene on your bulletin board complete with trapeze artists, clowns, lions, and high-wire performers. If you prefer, show several circus wagons with animals peering out or design clown faces for your board. Cut out posters in the shape of a tent, clown, or circus wagon or design a poster featuring a lion with his mouth open and program information written inside. Decorate handouts with a clown or with elephants joined tail to trunk. You can create handouts that resemble admission tickets to the circus.

PROGRAM PLAN

Lend a festive circus atmosphere to your program area with colored flags, banners, and streamers. You might like to wear a ringmaster's hat.

Introduction

Introduce the program: "Have you ever been to a circus? Do you know what you see there? There's a ringmaster who introduces the acts as well as clowns, lions, elephants, tightrope walkers, jugglers, trapeze artists, bears, and many other animals and performers."

Poetry

Circus by Jack Prelutsky. il. by Arnold Lobel. New York: Macmillan, [1974]. unpaged.
Introduce the poems: "Let's take a peek at the circus taking place inside this book. It will give you a better idea of the sights and sounds of a circus."
Share the following selections with the children: "Over and over the tumblers tumble," "Eight big black bears six feet tall," "Bring on the clowns," and "Here come the animals, ten feet high."

Read Aloud

Donkey's Dreadful Day by Irina Hale. il. by author. New York: Atheneum, 1982.
Introduce the story: "Donkey decides that he wants to be the cook for the circus. He thinks he'll be able to eat carrots all day long if he's in charge of the food. But, when the cook lets Donkey take over his job, Donkey discovers that it's not so easy to prepare meals for and serve all the animals and people in the circus."

Fingerplay

"Bears Everywhere," p. 53 in *Ring a Ring O' Roses: Stories, Games and Finger Plays for Pre-School Children*, rev. ed. Flint, Mich.: Flint Public Library, 1981.
Introduce the fingerplay: "Bears perform tricks in many circuses. Let's share a story about some of their antics now."

Because this is an easy rhyme to learn with simple actions, have the children join you immediately and then repeat it.

Bears Everywhere

Bears, bears, bears, everywhere!	(Point in all directions.)
Bears climbing stairs,	(Pretend to climb.)
Bears sitting on chairs,	(Pretend to sit.)
Bears collecting fares,	(Reach out for fares— place hands in pockets.)
Bears giving stares.	(Stare at group.)
Bears washing hairs,	(Pretend to wash hair.)
Bears, bears, bears, everywhere!	

Read Aloud

Little Bear and the Papagini Circus by Margaret Greaves. il. by Francesca Crespi. New York: Dial Books for Young Readers, 1986.

Introduce the story: "Little Bear is disappointed. His brother, sister, mother, and father perform in the Papagini Circus but Little Bear is too small to join them. He gets into a lot of trouble when he tries the family's acts, and his mother warns him that he must be quiet during the show. Will Little Bear be quiet or will he get into mischief?"

Fingerplay

"This Little Clown," p. 54 in *Ring a Ring O' Roses: Stories, Games, and Finger Plays for Pre-School Children*, rev. ed. Flint, Mich.: Flint Public Library, 1981.

Introduce the fingerplay: "What's a circus without the clowns? Here comes a parade of them now. Let's count them."

This counting fingerplay is very easy to do, so try it twice with the children.

This Little Clown

This little clown is fat and gay;	(Hold up thumb.)
This little clown does tricks all day;	(Hold up pointer finger.)
This little clown is tall and strong;	(Hold up middle finger.)
This little clown sings a funny song;	(Hold up ring finger and wiggle it.)
This little clown is wee and small	(Hold up little finger.)
But he can do anything at all.	

Read Aloud

Henry Explores the Jungle by Mark Taylor. il. by Graham Booth. New York: Atheneum, 1968.

Introduce the story: "When Henry and his dog Laird Angus McAngus pretend to explore the jungle their adventure involves them with a circus animal and a trip to the circus. Let's see how."

Read Aloud

Lyle and Humus by Jane Breskin Zalben. il. by author. New York: Macmillan, 1974.

Introduce the story: "Meet close friends Lyle, the monkey, and Humus, the elephant. They do everything together including their circus act. But something happens that makes them stop talking to each other. Will they ever be friends again?"

Action Rhyme

"Tightrope Walker," p. 54 in *Ring a Ring O' Roses: Stories, Games and Finger Plays for Pre-School Children*, rev. ed. Flint, Mich.: Flint Public Library, 1981.

Introduce the fingerplay: "We've met tumblers, bears, clowns, and tigers, and now let's pretend that we're tightrope walkers. Be careful. We're high in the air."

The actions in this rhyme are simple so do it with the children without demonstrating. Repeat.

Tightrope Walker

While the band is playing,   (Suit actions to words.)
Back and forth I go.
High above the people,
Sitting far below.
While the crowd is cheering,
I sway from side to side.
Now my act is over,
Down the pole I slide.

Participation Activity

"Clown Faces." Developed by the children's staff of the Thomas Crane Public Library, Quincy, Massachusetts.

Introduce the activity: "A short time ago we counted circus clowns. Now let's make clown faces."

Do Ahead: Using felt, design and cut out head shapes, hair pieces, eyes, noses, mouths, and collars to create clown faces.

During the program: Invite each child in turn to add a feature to the clown. Do this several times with different head shapes so each child has at least one turn.

You might like to give each child a small bag of peanuts or popcorn to take home as a souvenir from "circus stories."

TRY THIS!

Read Aloud

Aiken, Amy. *Wanda's Circus*. il. by author. Scarsdale, N.Y.: Bradbury Press, 1985.

Barton, Byron. *Harry is a Scaredy Cat*. il. by author. New York: Macmillan, 1974.

Gantos, Jack. *Rotten Ralph*. il. by Nicole Rubel. Boston: Houghton Mifflin, 1976.

Gay, Michel. *Night Ride*. il. by author. New York: William Morrow, 1986.

Modell, Frank. *Seen Any Cats?* il. by author. New York: Greenwillow, 1979.

Petersham, Maud, and Misha Petersham. *Circus Baby*. il. by authors. New York: Macmillan, 1950.

Thaler, Mike. *The Clown's Smile*. il. by Tracey Cameron. New York: Harper & Row, 1986.

Book Talk

Anno, Mitsumasa. *Dr. Anno's Magical Midnight Circus*. il. by author. New York: John Weatherhill, 1971.

Brown, Marc. *Lenny and Lola*. il. by author. New York: E. P. Dutton, 1978.

Freeman, Don. *Bearymore*. il. by author. New York: Viking Press, 1976.

Peppé, Rodney. *Circus Numbers: A Counting Book*. il. by author. New York: Delacorte Press, 1969. (This book lends itself to a creative dramatics activity.)

Piatti, Celestino, and Ursula Huber. *The Nock Family Circus*. translated from the German by Barbara Kowal Gollob. New York: Atheneum, 1968.

Rey, Hans Augusto. *Curious George Rides a Bike*. Boston: Houghton Mifflin, 1952.

Wildsmith, Brian. *Brian Wildsmith's Circus*. il. by author. New York: Franklin Watts, 1970.

Other Story Forms

"The Circus," pp. 28-29 in *Tell and Draw Stories* by Margaret J. Olson. Minneapolis, Minn.: Creative Storytime Press, 1963.

"Penny at the Circus," pp. 10-12 in *Kidstuff*, vol. 1, no. 2, "Razzle Dazzle Circus" edited by Sheila Debs. Lake Park, Fla.: GuideLines Press, 1981.

Poetry

"Holding Hands," p. 11 by Lenore M. Link in *Read-Aloud Rhymes for the Very Young* selected by Jack Prelutsky. il. by Marc Brown. New York: Alfred A. Knopf, 1986.

Fingerplay and Action Rhyme

"The Circus," p. 100 in *Let's Do Fingerplays* by Marion F. Grayson. il. by Nancy Weyl. Washington, D.C.: Robert B. Luce, 1962.

"The Circus Clown," in *My Big Book of Fingerplays: A Fun-to-Say, Fun-to-Play Collection* by Daphne Hogstrom. il. by Sally Augustiny. Racine, Wis.: Western Publishing, 1974. unpaged.

"An Elephant Goes Like This and That," p. 14 in *Games for the Very Young: Finger Plays and Nursery Rhymes* compiled by Elizabeth Matterson. New York: American Heritage Press/McGraw Hill, 1971.

"Monkey See-Monkey Do," p. 53 and "Monkey Song," and "Pretending," p. 54 in *Ring a Ring O' Roses: Stories, Games and Finger Plays for Pre-School Children*, rev. ed. Flint, Mich.: Flint Public Library, 1981.

"My Circus Balloon," and "Ten Little Clowns," p. 4, "Ten Circus Wagons," p. 5 and "What Do We See at the Circus?" and "The Puppet Clown," p. 6 in *Kidstuff*, vol. 1, no. 2, "Razzle Dazzle Circus" edited by Sheila Debs. Lake Park, Fla.: GuideLines Press, 1981.

Song

"The Circus Band," p. 7 in *Kidstuff*, vol. 1, no. 2, "Razzle Dazzle Circus" edited by Sheila Debs. Lake Park, Fla.: GuideLines Press, 1981.

Filmstrip

Curious George Rides a Bike. Weston, Conn.: Weston Woods, n.d. 10 min.

Film

Balthazar the Lion. Ossining, N.Y.: Wombat Productions, 1973. 12 min.

Curious George Rides a Bike. Weston, Conn.: Weston Woods, 1958. 10 min.

Activities

"Follow the Ringmaster," and "Move Like Different Circus Animals," p. 202 in *Everyday Circle Times* by Liz and Dick Wilmes. il. by Jeane Healy. Dundee, Ill.: Building Blocks, 1983.

Meet My Family

PUBLICITY

Glue large and small paper dolls on your posters to represent family members. Excellent instructions for making paper dolls in a ring or in a strip are found on p. 309 in *Handbook for Storytellers* by Caroline Feller Bauer. Chicago: American Library Association, 1977. Use the same idea on your handouts or turn your handouts into picture frames with smiling faces, young and old, that represent family members. Arrange photographs of your family members and those of other staff members on a bulletin board. If you prefer, depict animal families on your bulletin board, show a mother duck with her ducklings on your handouts, and decorate your posters with a mother rabbit and her babies.

PROGRAM PLAN

Display framed pictures of your family in the program area. Children are particularly interested in old photographs which show clothing, accessories, and hairstyles of an earlier time.

Introduction

Introduce the program: "There are all kinds of families, large and small—families with a mother or father, families with a mom and a dad, families with one child or many children. A family can also include cousins, aunts, uncles, grandmothers and grandfathers, or close family friends who are just like family. Whatever size your family is you probably love one another very much and do many things together. That's what the families are like in the stories we'll share today."

Read Aloud

Hazel's Amazing Mother by Rosemary Wells. il. by author. New York: Dial
  Books for Young Readers, 1985.
  Introduce the story: "Hazel buys some goodies so she and her mother can have a picnic, but Hazel gets lost on the way home. Some unkind children find Hazel and ruin something she cares about very much. I'm sure that Hazel's mother won't let these naughty children get away with that."

Song

"Jack and Jill," p. 39 in *Singing Bee! A Collection of Favorite Children's
  Songs* compiled by Jane Hart. il. by Anita Lobel. New York: Lothrop,
  Lee & Shepard Books, 1982.
  For verses two and three see "Jack and Jill, p. 52 in *Let's Do Fingerplays*
  by Marion F. Grayson. il. by Nancy Weyl. Washington, D.C.: Robert B.
  Luce, 1962.
  Introduce the song: "Do you know the song about Jack and Jill? Did you know that they were brother and sister? Listen carefully to the whole song and you'll hear about it."
  Have the children sing the first verse with you since many of them will know it. Sing the second and third verses and then repeat the entire song.

Read Aloud

Arthur's Baby by Marc Brown. il. by author. Boston: Joy Street/Little,
    Brown, 1987.
    Introduce the story: "Do you have a baby in the family? Do you like him
or her? Maybe you were happy when you heard that you'd have a baby brother
or sister. Arthur isn't happy about it. He worries that the baby will be like his
sister, D.W. Will he like the baby when she comes home? Will he know how to
help with the baby? Let's find out the answers together."

Book Talk

Avocado Baby by John Burningham. il. by author. New York: Thomas Y.
    Crowell, 1982.
    Introduce the story: "In this story you'll meet Mr. and Mrs. Hargraves
and their two children. They are not very strong people. When Mrs. Hargraves
has a baby it doesn't like to eat much and it doesn't get strong either. Mrs. Hargraves doesn't know what to do but after trying everything else she gives the
baby an avocado pear to eat. Amazing things begin to happen then."

Fingerplay

"Families" by Paula Gaj Sitarz.
    Introduce the fingerplay. "Families do have a lot of fun together. They go
on picnics, for walks, to the movies, shopping.... They play games like
marbles and 'Go Fish.' They play sports like baseball, swimming, and biking.
Sometimes families have get-togethers where they laugh and sing, eat and tell
jokes.
    Often you do things separately with one person in your family. Here's a
story about a young person who does special activities with different members
of her family. It's a story rhyme we can do together."
    This rhyme can be done seated. There are many actions in this rhyme so
demonstrate it first. Then invite the children to join you. Repeat.

Families

My family is so much fun.
There's lots to do with everyone.
(Open arms wide.)

With Mommy I like to mow the lawn.
(Pretend to place hands on mower handles. Push.)

With Uncle Josh I row on the pond.
(Rowing motion with arms.)

With Daddy I wash and wax the car.
(Pretend to squirt hose.)

With Cousin I jump and run so far.
(Jump one hand over other. Run middle and index finger.)

With Sister I throw and catch a ball.
(Imitate throwing and catching a ball.)

With Baby I feed and rock the doll.
(Pretend to feed and rock doll.)

Times we're together are the best, you bet.
I know *you'd* agree if we ever met.
(Point to children.)

Read Aloud

My Dad the Magnificent by Kristy Parker. il. by Lillian Hoban. New York: E. P. Dutton, 1987.
Introduce the story: "When Alex brags about his dad, Buddy feels he has to tell Alex how great *his* father is. Buddy tells some wild stories about his dad. But, the truth is, Buddy's dad isn't special because he does outrageous, heroic, or daring deeds. Buddy's dad is special for other reasons."

Read Aloud

All in One Piece by Jill Murphy. il. by author. New York: Putnam, 1987.
Introduce the story: "All mother elephant wants is to get dressed up for an evening out, without the children messing her clothing or her hair. Is it possible?"

Book Talk

Molly Pink by Judith Caseley. il. by author. New York: Greenwillow, 1985.
Introduce the story: "Molly is picked to sing a solo in the class concert. Oh, how she practices—in the bathtub, in bed, everywhere. When Molly tries to sing in the living room, however, she can't, not with her family watching. What will Molly do the night of the concert with her family watching from the audience? Will she be able to sing?"

Bailey Goes Camping by Kevin Henkes. il. by author. New York: Greenwillow, 1985.
Introduce the story: "Bailey's brother and sister Bruce and Betty are going camping, but Bailey is too young to go. Bailey has to stay home and he's not happy about that. He wants to go camping. What to do? Mom has an idea. Bailey can camp at home. Share this book with someone at home and find out how Bailey camps indoors."

Piggybook by Anthony Browne. il. by author. New York: Alfred A. Knopf, 1986.
Introduce the story: "The Piggots, Mr. Piggot, Simon, and Patrick, take Mrs. Piggot for granted. She does everything around the house—cooks meals, does the laundry, vacuums—and they do nothing. Is that fair? Can Mrs. Piggot do anything about this situation?"

Filmstrip

Benjamin and Tulip by Rosemary Wells. il. by author. Weston, Conn.: Weston Woods, 1975. 4 min.

Introduce the filmstrip: "Poor Benjamin. Everytime he tries to go to the store for his Aunt Fern, his cousin Tulip bothers him. Benjamin always gets blamed. What can Benjamin do to get Tulip to stop bothering him?"

Participation Story

"The Shopping Trip," p. 37 in *Ring a Ring O' Roses: Stories, Games and Finger Plays for Pre-School Children*, rev. ed. Flint, Mich.: Flint Public Library, 1981.

Introduce the story: "Do you ever go shopping with your family? It can be a lot of fun. Let's go now."

Try this with the children doing one motion at a time. Repeat. Then try it as suggested, continuing each motion as you add another.

The Shopping Trip

We're going on a shopping trip	(Name a local store.)
In a big department store.	
We're going to buy a pair of scissors first.	(Cutting motion with forefinger and middle finger of right hand.)
We need a new set of steps for the back porch.	(Walking step motion with feet.)
There was a sale of rocking chairs,	(Rocking motion back and forth while walking with feet and
So we bought one.	cutting with fingers.)
We got thirsty walking around	(Make lump in cheek with
And bought some bubble gum.	tongue and begin chewing.)
At this moment our heads began to itch.	(Scratch heads while continuing previous motions.)
The salesman came up to us and asked	(Shake head from side to side still continuing all the
If we wanted to buy anything else.	motion.)

TRY THIS!

Read Aloud

Aliki. *Jack and Jake*. il. by author. New York: Greenwillow, 1986.

Brandenburg, Franz. *I Wish I Was Sick, Too*. il. by Aliki. New York: Greenwillow, 1976.

Brandenburg, Franz. *A Secret for Grandmother's Birthday*. il. by Aliki. New York: Greenwillow, 1975.

Douglass, Barbara. *Good as New*. il. by Patience Brewster. New York: Lothrop, Lee & Shepard Books, 1982.

Greaves, Margaret. *Little Bear and the Papagini Circus*. il. by Francesca Crespi. New York: Dial Books for Young Readers, 1986.

Hayes, Sarah. *Eat Up, Gemma*. il. by Jan Ormerod. New York: Lothrop, Lee & Shepard Books, 1988.

Hutchins, Pat. *The Doorbell Rang*. il. by author. New York: Greenwillow, 1986.

Keats, Ezra Jack. *Peter's Chair*. il. by author. New York: Harper & Row, 1967.

Kellogg, Steven. *Much Bigger than Martin*. il. by author. New York: Dial Press, 1976.

McPhail, David. *Something Special*. il. by author. Boston: Little, Brown, 1988.

Murphy, Jill. *Five Minutes' Peace*. il. by author. New York: Putnam, 1986.

Preston, Edna Mitchell. *Where Did My Mother Go?* il. by Chris Conover. New York: Four Winds Press, 1978.

Rayner, Mary. *Mrs. Pig's Bulk Buy*. il. by author. New York: Atheneum, 1981.

Rice, Eve. *Ebbie*. il. by author. New York: Greenwillow, 1975.

Spier, Peter. *Oh, Were They Ever Happy!* il. by author. Garden City, N.Y.: Doubleday, 1978.

Titherington, Jean. *A Place for Ben*. il. by author. New York: Greenwillow, 1987.

Zolotow, Charlotte. *If It Weren't for You*. il. by Ben Schecter. New York: Harper & Row, 1966.

Book Talk

Ackerman, Karen. *Song and Dance Man*. il. by Stephen Gammell. New York: Alfred A. Knopf, 1988.

Alexander, Martha. *I'll Be the Horse If You'll Play with Me*. il. by author. New York: Dial Press, 1975.

Alexander, Martha. *Nobody Asked Me If I Wanted a Baby Sister*. il. by author. New York: Dial Books for Young Readers, 1971.

Bauer, Caroline Feller. *My Mom Travels a Lot*. il. by Nancy Winslow Parker. New York: Frederick Warne, 1981.

Cazets, Denys. *Great-Uncle Felix*. il. by author. New York: Orchard Books, 1988.

Daly, Niki. *Not So Fast Songololo*. il. by author. New York: Atheneum, 1986.

Hazen, Barbara Shook. *Even If I Did Something Awful.* il. by Nancy Kincade. New York: Atheneum, 1981.

Hughes, Shirley. *An Evening at Alfie's.* il. by author. New York: Lothrop, Lee & Shepard Books, 1984.

Mosel, Arlene. *Tikki Tikki Tembo.* il. by Blair Lent. New York: Holt, Rinehart, and Winston, 1968.

Rice, Eve. *New Blue Shoes.* il. by author. New York: Macmillan, 1975.

Rylant, Cynthia. *The Relatives Came.* il. by Stephen Gammell. Scarsdale, N.Y.: Bradbury Press, 1985.

Schwartz, Amy. *Her Majesty, Aunt Essie.* il. by author. Scarsdale, N.Y.: Bradbury Press, 1984.

Steig, William. *Sylvester and the Magic Pebble.* il. by author. New York: Windmill Books, 1969.

Wells, Rosemary. *Good Night, Fred.* il. by author. New York: Dial Press, 1981.

Wells, Rosemary. *Noisy Nora.* il. by author. New York: Dial Books for Young Readers, 1973.

Williams, Barbara. *Kevin's Grandma.* il. by Kay Chorao. New York: E. P. Dutton, 1975.

Poetry

"Brother," p. 52 by Mary Ann Hoberman in *Tomie dePaola's Book of Poems.* il. by Tomie dePaola. New York: Putnam, 1988.

"Little Pictures," p. 43 by Arnold Lobel in *The Read-Aloud Treasury* compiled by Joanna Cole and Stephanie Calmenson. il. by Ann Schweninger. Garden City, N.Y.: Doubleday, 1988.

Fingerplay and Action Rhyme

"How Many," p. 29 in *Clap Your Hands: Finger Rhymes* chosen by Sarah Hayes. il. by Toni Goffe. New York: Lothrop, Lee & Shepard Books, 1988.

Filmstrip

Noisy Nora by Rosemary Wells. Weston, Conn.: Weston Woods, 1975. 10 min.

Activities

"Family Chores." A creative dramatics activity developed by Paula Gaj Sitarz. Below are some family chores the children can act out:

- Wash and dry the dishes.

- Sweep the floor.

- Clean the windows.

- Throw out the garbage.

- Rake leaves.

- Mow the lawn.

- Wash the wheels on the car.

- Vacuum the rug.

- Put clothes in the dryer.

- Get the mail from the mailbox.

- Dust the furniture.

- Set the table for a meal.

- Put toys away in the toy box.

- Feed the pet.

- Water the plants.

Getting Together:
Stories about Friends

This program can be used as is, as a Valentine's Day program, or in combination with Valentine's Day stories.

PUBLICITY

Hands joined together or smiling faces can be used to decorate handouts and posters. You have several options for decorating your bulletin board. Show two children playing on a seesaw. Trace hands on construction paper and then tack pairs of hands or a ring of hands on the board. Perhaps you have photographs of children wearing national costumes. If you like, use pictures — book jackets or drawn free hand — of friends found in books. Include George and Martha, Frog and Toad, Corduroy and Lisa and any other book friends you think the children will recognize.

PROGRAM PLAN

Read Aloud

Friends by Satomi Ichikawa. il. by author. New York: Parents Magazine Press, 1977.
    Introduce the story: "Do you have friends? They can be a lot of fun, can't they. What else is a friend? Let's share this short story and see what the writer of this book says about friends."

Read Aloud

Ira Sleeps Over by Bernard Waber. il. by author. Boston: Houghton Mifflin, 1972.
    Introduce the story: "Meet two good friends, Reggie and Ira. Reggie and Ira can have a great time when Ira sleeps over at Reggie's house. They can have pillow fights and tell scary stories. They can eat snacks and play games. But Ira may not have a good time if he can't decide whether or not to bring his teddy bear to Reggie's."

Fingerplay

"Two Little Houses Across the Street," p. 168, author unknown, in *Channels to Children: Early Childhood Activity Guide for Holidays and Seasons* by Carol Beckman, Roberta Simmons, and Nancy Thomas. il. by Debbie Reisbeck. Colorado Springs, Colo.: Channels to Children, 1982.
    Introduce the fingerplay: "Let's meet two other friends who like to play together."
    This is an easy finger rhyme to do so have the children join you immediately. Repeat.

"Two Little Houses Across the Street"

Two little houses across the street,
(Two fists.)

Open the doors and then friends meet.
(Open fists.)

How do you do? How do you do?
(Move one finger on one hand and then index finger on the other hand.)

Such nice, sunny weather
(Form circle in air.)

Off they hurried to the park
Two little friends together.
(Make fingers on two hands walk.)

Fingerplay

"Josh and Sue and Tim and Kate" by Paula Gaj Sitarz.
　　Introduce the fingerplay: "Let's meet four more friends who have fun together."
　　Demonstrate this first before you invite the children to join you. Repeat.

"Josh and Sue and Tim and Kate"

Josh and Sue and Tim and Kate
(Hold up finger for each name.)

Like to play outside.
They climb the trees,
(Move fists higher one over the other.)

They slide and swing,
(Swing arms.)

And everyday they hide.
(Cover face with hands.)

They bump and roll and all fall down.
(Bump fists. Roll open hands. Collapse open hands over each other.)

But soon the hour is late.
And now it's time to wave goodbye,
(Wave.)

For Josh, Sue, Tim, and Kate.
(Hold up one finger for each name.)

Read Aloud

A Porcupine Named Fluffy by Helen Lester. il. by Lynn Munsinger. Boston: Houghton Mifflin,1986.
　　Introduce the story: "Poor Fluffy the porcupine. His name doesn't fit him

at all. With his sharp quills, there's nothing soft about him. Fluffy does everything he can to live up to his name, but nothing works. He's so sad until he meets someone else whose name doesn't fit him either."

Read Aloud

Corduroy by Don Freeman. il. by author. New York: Viking Press, 1968.
   Introduce the story: "Corduroy is a soft, furry, cuddly teddy bear who lives in a department store. What he wishes for more than anything is that someone buy him, take him home, and be his friend."

Song

"The More We Get Together," pp. 52-53 in *The Raffi Singable Songbook: A Collection of 51 Songs from Raffi's First Three Records for Young Children.* il. by Joyce Yamamoto. New York: Crown, 1987.
   Introduce the song: "The friends in the stories we've shared so far have a good time. Getting together is fun and here's a song we can share that talks about that."
   This is an easy song to learn so begin the song and invite the children to sing too. Repeat as long as everyone is interested.

Puppetry

George and Martha by James Marshall. il. by author. Boston: Houghton Mifflin, 1972.
   Introduce the stories: "The hippos George and Martha are best friends but sometimes they do things that upset each other."

   "Split Pea Soup," pp. 5-13.
   Introduce the story: "Martha is always making split pea soup for George. Let's find out if he likes her soup."
   You will need George and Martha puppets and the following props: a table, a soup bowl, shoes, and chocolate chip cookies.

   "The Mirror," pp. 31-37.
   Introduce the story: "George is tired of Martha staring at herself in the mirror. What can he do about it?"
   You will need George and Martha puppets and the following props: a mirror and a mirror with an ugly face on it.
   You can manipulate the puppets and the props by yourself or with an assistant. Use the book as a guide to making the puppets and props.

Participation Book

Do You Want to Be My Friend? by Eric Carle. il. by author. New York: Thomas Y. Crowell, 1971.
   Introduce the book: "Let's join a mouse as he asks a number of animals to be his friend. We'll only see each animal's tail. Can you guess each of the animals to whom mouse is talking?"

Activities

Take photographs of the children in the story-hour group. Children love to have their pictures taken! A Polaroid camera is ideal because they can see themselves on film immediately. You can use the photographs for publicity for story hour. If you use a 110, disc, or 35mm camera, take at least one group photograph and make copies to give each child at the end of the series of story hours.

TRY THIS!

Read Aloud

Asch, Frank. *Bear's Bargain*. il. by author. Englewood Cliffs, N.J.: Prentice-Hall, 1985.

Cohen, Miriam. *Will I Have a Friend?* il. by Lillian Hoban. New York: Macmillan, 1967.

Delton, Judy. *Two Good Friends*. il. by Giulio Maestro. New York: Crown, 1974.

De Regniers, Beatrice Schenk. *May I Bring a Friend?* il. by Beni Montresor. New York: Atheneum, 1982.

Graham, Margaret Bloy. *Benjy and His Friend Fifi*. il. by author. New York: Harper & Row, 1988.

Keller, Holly. *Lizzie's Invitation*. il. by author. New York: Greenwillow, 1987.

Kent, Jack. *Joey*. il. by author. Englewood Cliffs, N.J.: Prentice-Hall, 1984.

Lionni, Leo. *Alexander and the Wind-Up Mouse*. il. by author. New York: Pantheon Books, 1969.

Lionni, Leo. *Little Blue and Little Yellow*. il. by author. New York: Ivan Obolensky, 1959.

Marshall, James. *The Guest*. il. by author. Boston: Houghton Mifflin, 1975.

Wildsmith, Brian. *The Lazy Bear*. il. by author. New York: Franklin Watts, 1974.

Book Talk

Aliki. *Overnight at Mary Bloom's*. il. by author. New York: Greenwillow, 1987.

Cohen, Miriam. *Best Friends*. il. by Lillian Hoban. New York: Macmillan, 1971.

Daugherty, James. *Andy and the Lion*. il. by author. New York: Viking Press, 1966.

Henkes, Kevin. *Chester's Way*. il. by author. New York: Greenwillow, 1988.

Holabird, Katharine. *Angelina and Alice*. il. by Helen Craig. New York: Clarkson N. Potter, 1987.

Keats, Ezra Jack. *Apt. 3*. il. by author. New York: Macmillan, 1971.

Kelly, Kathleen M. *River Friends*. il. by author. New York: Atheneum, 1988.

Sharmat, Marjorie Weinman. *The 329th Friend*. il. by Cyndy Szekeres. New York: Four Winds Press, 1979.

Zolotow, Charlotte. *My Friend John*. il. by Ben Shecter. New York: Harper & Row, 1968.

Poetry

"Noises," pp. 26-27 by Aileen Fisher in *Best Friends* poems selected by Lee Bennett Hopkins. il. by James Watts. New York: Harper & Row, 1986. This poem can be done as an action rhyme. Do the actions that the words suggest.

"We're Racing, Racing Down the Walk," p. 26 by Phyllis McGinley in *Tomie dePaola's Book of Poems*. il. by Tomie dePaola. New York: Putnam, 1988.

Fingerplay and Action Rhyme

"Playmates," p. 54 in *Let's Do Fingerplays* by Marion F. Grayson. il. by Nancy Weyl. Washington, D.C.: Robert B. Luce, 1962.

"Playmates," p. 69 in *Ring a Ring O' Roses: Stories, Games and Finger Plays for Pre-School Children*, rev. ed. Flint, Mich.: Flint Public Library, 1981.

Film

Little Blue and Little Yellow. New York: McGraw-Hill Films, 1962. 9 min.

On Logs and In Bogs:
Stories about Frogs

PUBLICITY

Cut out posters and handouts in the shape of a frog or a lily pad. Use photographs of frogs from back issues of *Your Big Backyard, Ranger Rick*, and *National Geographic World* on your bulletin board. Or tack paper lily pads to your board. What about a bulletin board decorated with children playing leap frog?

PROGRAM PLAN

Make lily pads out of felt for the children to sit on. Do you have access to a real frog to display in a terrarium? Arrange toy stuffed frogs like Kermit the Frog or Toad from *Wind in the Willows* in the story-hour space.

Introduction

Introduce the program: "Do you ever think about frogs? What do you know about them? They are usually shades of green or brown. They live in the water and on logs, rocks, and lily pads. And, according to the stories we'll share today, frogs lead interesting and exciting and sometimes dangerous lives."

Poem

"The Frog on the Log," p. 21 by Ilo Orleans in *Read-Aloud Rhymes for the Very Young* selected by Jack Prelutsky. il. by Marc Brown. New York: Alfred A. Knopf, 1986.
   Introduce the poem: "Watch what happens when a frog is chased by an owl."
   Share this poem on the felt board. You will need the following figures made of felt: a frog, a log, an owl, a tree, and a pond.

Read Aloud

The Mysterious Tadpole by Stephen Kellogg. il. by author. New York: Dial Press, 1977.
   Introduce the story: "Every year Uncle MacAllister gives Louis an interesting gift for his birthday. This year it's a tadpole. The teacher says it will grow into a frog, but Alphonse doesn't seem to be turning into an ordinary frog."

Fingerplay

"The Toad's Song," p. 30 in *Listen! And Help Tell the Story* by Bernice Wells Carlson. il. by Burmah Burris. Nashville, Tenn.: Abingdon, 1965.
   Introduce the fingerplay: "What's it like to be a frog? Let's share this rhyme and find out."
   Share this fingerplay with the children twice.

The Toad's Song*

(In this poem the right fist is the little toad which jumps about. Lay your fist flat on a table or in your lap. Curl your left hand around it, to make a little cell under the stone.)

I am a little toad Living by the road. Beneath a stone I dwell Snug in a little cell.	(Right fist rests quietly, sheltered by left hand.)
Hip, hip, hop. Hip, hip, hop!	(Move right fist up and down, behind left hand.)
Just listen to my song. I sleep all winter long	(Right hand is still.)

But in the spring I peep out
And then I jump about.
Hip, hip, hop.
Hip, hip, hop!
	(Move right fist from behind
	    left hand, and have it jump
	    about.)

And now I catch a fly Before he winks an eye.	(Make grabbing motion with right hand.)
And now I take a hop And now and then I stop. Hip, hip, hop. Hip, hip, hop! Stop!	(Making hopping motion until word "stop.")

Read Aloud

Frog's Holiday by Margaret Gordon. il. by author. New York: Viking Kestrel, 1986.

Introduce the story: "Meet some frogs who live in a busy, noisy, and threatening pond. What they need is a holiday. But finding the right place for a family of frogs to vacation is not easy."

Read Aloud

The Caterpillar and the Polliwog by Jack Kent. il. by author. Englewood Cliffs, N.J.: Prentice-Hall, 1982.

Introduce the story: "The caterpillar is so proud that it will grow and turn into a butterfly. The polliwog is equally impressed so it decides to watch the caterpillar and turn into a butterfly too. Let's see if it does."

Fingerplay

"Bullfrog," p. 4 in *Ring a Ring O' Roses: Stories, Games and Finger Plays Pre-School Children*, rev. ed. Flint, Mich.: Flint Public Library, 1981.

Introduce the fingerplay: "In the poem we shared about the frog on the log, the frog jumped into the pond when an owl chased him. What will Mr. Bullfrog do when a boy comes along?"

Demonstrate the fingerplay and then share it twice with the children.

---

*From *Listen! And Help Tell the Story* by Bernice Wells Carlson. Copyright © 1965 by Abingdon. Used by permission.

Bullfrog

Here's Mr. Bullfrog	(Left hand closed, thumb upright.)
Sitting on a rock	
Along comes a little boy,	(Walking motion with index and third fingers.)
Mr. Bullfrog jumps, KERPLOP!	(Thumb makes diving motion.)

Song

"Five Little Frogs," p. 28 by Lucille Wood and Louise Scott in *The Raffi Singable Songbook: A Collection of 51 Songs from Raffi's First Three Records for Young Children*. il. by Joyce Yamamoto. New York: Crown, 1987.

Introduce the song: "Let's meet five frogs who are having a wonderful time on a log, eating bugs and enjoying the cool pond."

Share this with the children on the felt board as you sing it with them. You will need the following felt pieces: five frogs, a log, and a pond.

This is a repetitive song which gives the children an opportunity to catch on and join in.

Participation Story

Jump, Frog, Jump by Robert Kalan. il. by Byron Barton. New York: Greenwillow, 1981.

Introduce the story: "How will frog escape the dangers awaiting him in and around the pond?"

Invite the children to join you on the refrain, "jump, frog, jump."

Film

A Boy, a Dog, and a Frog. New York: Phoenix Films & Video, Inc., 1980. 9 min.

Introduce the film: "What happens when a boy and his dog try to catch a frog? Is it an easy thing to do?"

Display the book: *A Boy, a Dog, and a Frog* by Mercer Mayer. il. by author. New York: Dial Press, 1967. (This is a wordless book.)

TRY THIS!

Read Aloud

Lionni, Leo. *Fish Is Fish*. il. by author. New York: Pantheon, 1970.

Lionni, Leo. *It's Mine! A Fable*. il. by author. New York: Alfred A. Knopf, 1986.

Wahl, Jan. *Doctor Rabbit's Foundling*. il. by Cyndy Szekeres. New York: Pantheon, 1977.

Book Talk

Duke, Kate. *Seven Froggies Went to School.* il. by author. New York: E. P. Dutton, 1985.

Mayer, Mercer. *Frog On His Own.* il. by author. New York: Dial Books for Young Readers, 1973. (This is a wordless book.)

Poetry

"A Big Turtle," p. 20 by Anonymous in *Read-Aloud Rhymes for the Very Young* selected by Jack Prelutsky. il. by Marc Brown. New York: Alfred A. Knopf, 1986.

"The Polliwog," p. 82 by Arthur Guiterman in *The Random House Book of Poetry for Children: A Treasury of 572 Poems for Today's Child* selected by Jack Prelutsky. il. by Arnold Lobel. New York: Random House, 1983.

Fingerplay and Action Rhyme

"Five Frisky Frogs," in *My Big Book of Finger Plays: A Fun-to-Say, Fun-to-Play Collection* by Daphne Hogstrom. il. by Sally Augustiny. Racine, Wis.: Western Publishing, 1974. unpaged.

"Five Little Froggies," p. 62 in *Let's Do Fingerplays* by Marion F. Grayson. il. by Nancy Weyl. Washington, D.C.: Robert B. Luce, 1962.

"The Frogs," p. 4 and "Frogs, Frogs, Frogs," p. 4 and "Mr. Frog," p. 5 in *Kidstuff*, vol. 3, no. 5, "Frog Fever" edited by Sheila Debs. Lake Park, Fla.: GuideLines Press, 1984.

"A Little Green Frog in a Pond Am I," a traditional poem adapted as a fingerplay by Paula Gaj Sitarz.

"A Little Green Frog in a Pond Am I"

A little green frog in a pond am I,
(Make fist with right hand. Hop fist in open palm of left hand.)

Hoppity, hoppity hop.
I sit on a little leaf, high and dry,
(Rest fist in open palm of left hand.)

And watch all the fishes as they swim by.
(With two hands together make swimming motions.)

Splash! How I make the water fly!
(Clap hands.)

Hoppity, hoppity hop.
(Make fist with right hand. Hop fist in open palm of left hand.)

"Ten Little Froggies," p. 44 and "Little Toad," p. 45 in *Finger Frolics: Over 250 Fingerplays for Children from 3 Years*, rev. ed. il. by Joan Lockwood. Livonia, Mich.: Partner Press, 1983.

"Three Little Leopard Frogs," p. 7 in *Ring a Ring O' Roses: Stories, Games and Finger Plays for Pre-School Children*, rev. ed. Flint, Mich.: Flint Public Library, 1981.

Song

The Foolish Frog by Pete and Charles Seeger. music adapted from an old song. book adapted and designed from Firebird Film by Gene Deitch. il. by Miroslav Jagr. New York: Macmillan, 1973.

"The Frog in the Bog," p. 134 in *Sally Go Round the Sun: Three Hundred Children's Rhymes, Songs and Games* by Edith Fowke. Garden City, N.Y.: Doubleday, 1969.

Filmstrip

Foolish Frog. Weston, Conn.: Weston Woods, 1974. 9 min.

Film

The Foolish Frog. Weston, Conn.: Weston Woods, 1973. 8 min.

How Does Your
Garden Grow?

PUBLICITY

Create handouts that look like seed packets or watering cans. Make posters or handouts shaped like carrots, tomatoes, strawberries, watermelons, onions, apples, or celery stalks. Decorate your bulletin board with a garden of vegetables or flowers, a basket of vegetables, or a variety of garden tools. Fashion them out of construction paper.

PROGRAM PLAN

Place a basket of vegetables near your seat or arrange some of the following items in the program area: a hand fork, rake, hoe, spade, garden hose, watering can, trowel, gloves, or seed packs. Wear a nursery apron, kneepads, or bib overalls and a straw or Panama hat. For a big effect place a scarecrow or wheelbarrow in the story-hour space.

Introduction

Introduce the program: "Have you ever grown anything in a garden? It's a lot of fun, but hard work too. What grew in the garden you tended? Let's see what's growing in the gardens we visit today."

Read Aloud

The Biggest Pumpkin Ever by Steven Kroll. il. by Jean Bassett. New York: Holiday House, 1984.

Introduce the story: "What would happen if two mice fell in love with the same tiny pumpkin and, without the other mouse knowing, each mouse worked very hard to help the pumpkin grow? How big might it become? And who would the pumpkin belong to?"

Book Talk

Pumpkin, Pumpkin by Jeanne Titherington. il. by author. New York: Greenwillow, 1986.

Introduce the story: "Share this book with someone at home and you can join Jamie as he plants a seed and watches it grow. Will his pumpkin grow as huge as the pumpkin the mice tended? What will Jamie do with his pumpkin?"

Fingerplay

"I Dig, Dig, Dig," p. 76 in *Ring a Ring O' Roses: Stories, Games and Finger Plays for Pre-School Children*, rev. ed. Flint, Mich.: Flint Public Library, 1981.

Introduce the fingerplay: "Let's plant seeds in our own garden. What will you grow?"

Do this slowly with the children. Repeat.

I Dig, Dig, Dig

I dig, dig, dig,	(Pretend to dig.)
And I plant some seeds.	(Stoop down and plant seeds.)
I rake, rake, rake,	(Pretend to rake.)
And I pull some weeds.	(Pull up weeds.)
I wait and watch	(Stoop down and watch ground intently.)
And soon I know	(Nod head.)
My garden sprouts	(Raise hands from ground as if sprouting.)
And starts to grow.	

Fingerplay

"Five Little Peas in a Pea Pod Pressed," p. 147 in *Channels to Children: Early Childhood Activity Guide for Holidays and Seasons* by Carol Beckman, Roberta Simmons and Nancy Thomas. il. by Debbie Reisbeck. Colorado Springs, Colo.: Channels to Children, 1982.

Introduce the fingerplay: "Have you ever thought about how peas grow? Let's share this story and find out together."

Try this easy fingerplay at least twice.

"Five Little Peas in a Pea Pod Pressed"

Five little peas in a pea pod pressed,
(Make fist.)

One grew, two grew, and so did the rest.
(Raise respective fingers.)

They grew and grew and did not stop
(Stretch fingers wide.)

Until one day the pod went POP!!
(Clap hands.)

Read Aloud

The Little Red Hen. il. by Paul Galdone. New York: The Seabury Press, 1973.

Introduce the story: "The mice we met in our first story were very willing to tend the pumpkin in the garden. But, in this story we'll meet a cat, a dog, and a mouse who don't like to do any work—not even the gardening. The little red hen who lives with them must do all the chores including the gardening. It isn't fair, and the little red hen decides to do something about it."

Read Aloud

The Turnip by Janina Domanska. il. by author. New York: Macmillan, 1969.

Introduce the story: "Grandfather plants a turnip. Grandmother waters it. But, when it's ready to harvest, they need help—and more help—because the turnip doesn't want to come out of the ground."

"In My Garden," pp. 79-80 in *The 2nd Raffi Songbook*. Piano arrangements by Catherine Ambrose. Design and illustrations by Joyce Yamamoto. New York: Crown, 1986.

Introduce the song: "We've read stories about gardening and we've pretended to garden. Now let's sing a song about growing plants."

Sing verses one through six. The tune is short and easy so the children will catch on quickly.

Felt-Board Story

Growing Vegetable Soup by Lois Ehlert. il. by author. San Diego, Calif.: Harcourt Brace Jovanovich, 1987.

Introduce the story: "Let's grow a garden of vegetables and turn them into soup."

You will need the following items cut out of felt: tools and seeds (which you might want to let the children put on the board), sprouts, a watering can, the sun, plants with leaves, fully grown plants, a cooking pot, and a bowl with soup in it.

Book Talk

Planting a Rainbow by Lois Ehlert. il. by author. San Diego, Calif.: Harcourt Brace Jovanovich, 1988.

Introduce the story: "Instead of planting vegetables you might enjoy planting a rainbow of flowers in your garden."

Book Talk

In My Garden: A Child's Gardening Book by Helen and Kelly Oechsli. il. by Kelly Oechsli. New York: Macmillan, 1985.

Introduce the story: "Would you like to have a garden in your yard or indoors? Share this book with an adult—they can read it, you can follow the directions—and you can have a wonderful and tasty vegetable garden. Wouldn't you like to plant lettuce, tomatoes, and zucchini?"

Activities

Plant Bean Seeds

Do Ahead: Fill paper cups two-thirds full with soil.

During the program: Give each child a paper "pot" filled with soil and four or five bean seeds to plant. Pass a watering can or a mister so each child can water his or her plant.

The children can either take their "pots" home or leave them at the program site to watch their progress week by week.

For further information see *Electric Company*. March 1984. p. 22 and *Your Big Backyard*. July 1983. p.19.

TRY THIS!

Read Aloud

Domanska, Janina. *The Best of the Bargain.* adapted from a Polish folktale. il. by author. New York: Greenwillow, 1977.

Hurd, Thatcher. *The Pea Patch Jig.* il. by author. New York: Greenwillow, 1986.

Krauss, Ruth. *The Carrot Seed.* il. by Crockett Johnson. New York: Harper & Row, 1945. (This short, easy-to-read book adapts well as a felt-board story.)

Nakagawa, Reiko. *A Blue Seed.* il. by Yuriko Omura. New York: Hastings House, 1967.

Rylant, Cynthia. *This Year's Garden.* il. by Mary Szilagyi. Scarsdale, N.Y.: Bradbury Press, 1984.

Tolstoy, Alexei. *The Great Big Enormous Turnip.* il. by Helen Oxenbury. New York: Franklin Watts, 1968. (This story adapts well as a felt-board story.)

Westcott, Nadine Bernard. *The Giant Vegetable Garden.* il. by author. Boston: Little, Brown, 1981.

Book Talk

Aliki. *The Story of Johnny Appleseed.* il. by author. Englewood Cliffs, N.J.: Prentice-Hall, 1963.

Balian, Lorna. *A Garden for a Groundhog.* il. by author. Nashville, Tenn.: Abingdon, 1985.

Carle, Eric. *The Tiny Seed.* il. by author. New York: Thomas Y. Crowell, 1970.

Le Tord, Bijou. *Rabbit Seeds.* il. by author. New York: Four Winds Press, 1984.

McMillan, Bruce. *Growing Colors.* photographs by author. New York: Lothrop, Lee & Shepard Books, 1988.

Moore, Inga. *The Vegetable Thieves.* il. by author. New York: Viking Press, 1983.

Rockwell, Harlow. *The Compose Heap.* il. by author. Garden City, N.Y.: Doubleday, 1974.

Other Story Forms

"The Turnip," pp. 50-55 and "The Goat in the Turnip Field," pp. 64-68 in *The Flannel Board Storytelling Book* by Judy Sierra. Chicago: H. W. Wilson, 1987.

Poetry

"Little Seeds," by Else Holmelund Minarik and "A Spike of Green," by Barbara Baker, p. 14 in *Read-Aloud Rhymes for the Very Young* selected by Jack Prelutsky. il. by Marc Brown. New York: Alfred A. Knopf, 1986.

"Mary, Mary, Quite Contrary," p. 62 in *Tomie dePaola's Mother Goose*. il. by Tomie dePaola. New York: Putnam, 1985.

Fingerplay and Action Rhyme

"Dig a Little Hole," in *Little Boy Blue: Finger Plays Old and New* by Daphne Hogstrom. il. by Alice Schlesinger. Racine, Wis.: Western Publishing, 1966. unpaged.

"Farmer Plows the Ground," p. 76 and "Trees," p. 78 in *Ring a Ring O' Roses: Stories, Games and Finger Plays for Pre-School Children*, rev. ed. Flint, Mich.: Flint Public Library, 1981.

"Five Fat Peas," p. 19 in *Clap Your Hands: Finger Rhymes* chosen by Sarah Hayes. il. by Toni Goffe. New York: Lothrop, Lee & Shepard Books, 1988.

"Flower Garden," p. 45 in *Finger Plays and Action Rhymes* by Frances E. Jacobs. photographs by Lura and Courtney Owen. New York: Lothrop, Lee & Shepard Books, 1941.

"Growing," in *My Big Book of Fingerplays: A Fun-to-Say, Fun-to-Play Collection* by Daphne Hogstrom. il. by Sally Augustiny. Racine, Wis.: Western Publishing, 1974. unpaged.

"I Dig a Hole and Plant a Seed," p. 146 in *Channels to Children: Early Childhood Activity Guide for Holidays and Seasons* by Carol Beckman, Roberta Simmons, and Nancy Thomas. il. by Debbie Reisbeck. Colorado Springs, Colo.: Channels to Children, 1982.

"My Flower Garden," p. 103 by C. S. Peterson in *Story Programs: A Source Book of Materials* by Carolyn Sue Peterson and Brenny Hall. Metuchen, N.J.: Scarecrow Press, 1980.

"My Garden," p. 46 in *Let's Do Fingerplays* by Marion F. Grayson. il. by Nancy Weyl. Washington, D.C.: Robert. B. Luce, 1962.

"The Rainbow," p. 32, "Little Brown Seed," p. 33 and "Planting a Bean," p. 54 in *Finger Frolics: Over 250 Fingerplays for Children from 3 Years*, rev. ed. il. by Joan Lockwood. Livonia, Mich.: Partner Press, 1983.

Song

"The Gardner Plants the Seeds," p. 160 in *Channels to Children: Early Childhood Activity Guide for Holidays and Seasons* by Carol Beckman, Roberta Simmons, and Nancy Thomas. il. by Debbie Reisbeck. Colorado Springs, Colo.: Channels to Children, 1982.

"Mistress Mary," p. 38 in *Singing Bee! A Collection of Favorite Children's Songs.* compiled by Jane Hart. il. by Anita Lobel. New York: Lothrop, Lee & Shepard Books, 1982.

"Oats and Beans and Barley," pp. 13-14 in *The 2nd Raffi Songbook.* piano arrangements by Catherine Ambrose. design and illustration by Joyce Yamamoto. New York: Crown, 1986.

"Planting Corn," p. 6 in *Kidstuff*, vol. 4, no. 8, "Vegetable Jamboree" edited by Sheila Debs. Lake Park, Fla.: GuideLines Press, 1987.

Films

The Mole and the Bulldozer. New York: Phoenix Films & Video, 1975. 7 min.

The Mole and the Gardener. New York: Phoenix Films & Video, 1974. 9 min.

Activities

"Garden Tools Shadow Game" developed by Paula Gaj Sitarz.
Select an assortment of garden tools and hold one up at a time behind a screen which is illuminated by a lamp. Ask the children to identify each garden tool or accessory based on its shadow. You might include: a hoe, rake, glove, watering can, trowel, piece of hose, and a straw hat.

"Planting Pantomime," p. 153 in *Channels to Children: Early Childhood Activity Guide for Holidays and Seasons* by Carol Beckman, Roberta Simmons, and Nancy Thomas. il. by Debbie Reisbeck. Colorado Springs, Colo.: Channels to Children, 1982.

"What's Missing?" p. 5 in *Kidstuff*, vol. 4, no. 8, "Vegetable Jamboree" edited by Sheila Debs. Lake Park, Fla.: GuideLines Press, 1987.

What's on Top?
Stories about Hats

PUBLICITY

Create posters and handouts in the shape of a hat. Use your imagination and create any fanciful hat you like. A mixture of hats cut out of construction paper and felt make a colorful bulletin board. If you like, depict a hat rack holding hats associated with different professions.

PROGRAM PLAN

Fill the program area with as many types of hats as you can find. These might include a bicycle helmet, a wedding veil, a beret, a ski cap, a bathing cap, a shower cap, a baseball cap, and a birthday hat. Do you have a hat rack to put the hats on? Be sure to wear your favorite hat (at least to begin the program).

Introduction

Introduce the program: "Hats! So many people wear them. Many hats tell you what a person does for a living or they tell you what a person is like. In many of the stories we'll share today, hats just don't want to stay on anyone's head. Some of the hats are very unusual, unlike any you've ever seen."

Read Aloud

Martin's Hats by Joan W. Blos. il. by Marc Simont. New York: William Morrow, 1984.
  Introduce the story: "There are special hats for all kinds of jobs. When you put on any of those hats you can have a great adventure, as Martin discovers."

Read Aloud

Olive and the Magic Hat by Eileen Christelow. il. by author. New York: Clarion Books/Ticknor & Fields, 1987.
  Introduce the story: "It's Father's birthday and Mother has bought him a tall black hat. Olive and her brother Otis are told not to touch the hat. Do they listen to Mother? No, and this is what happens."

Fingerplay

"Hat Woes" by Paula Gaj Sitarz.
  Introduce the fingerplay: "Hats don't always stay on your head the way you want them to. That's what happens in this finger rhyme."
  There are many actions in this rhyme so demonstrate and then have the children join you. Repeat.

Hat Woes

I put a hat on my head,
(Pretend to put a hat on your head.)

But it covered my face.
(Pull hand down from top of head over face.)

I put another hat on,
(Put hat on head.)

But it wouldn't stay in place.
(Adjust hat with hands.)

The next hat was red,
(Put hat on head.)

It popped off my head.
(Hand flies off head into air.)

The last hat was straw,
(Put hat on head.)

The wind blew it far.
(Wave arm in the air.)

So next time you try to cover your head,
Remember what happened to me.
(Point to self.)

It's not so easy to wear a hat,
(Shake finger.)

For hats just want to be free!
(Open arms wide.)

Read Aloud

The Quangle Wangle's Hat by Edward Lear. il. by Janet Stevens. New York: Harcourt Brace Jovanovitch, 1988.
   Introduce the story: "In a tree lives the Quangle Wangle with a hat perched atop its head. The 102-inch wide hat can be seen for miles around and soon all sorts of strange creatures come to make their home in the hat. Let's meet the creatures now. They include the Fimble Fowl, the Pobble, and the Attery Squash."

Felt-Board Story

Caps for Sale by Esphyr Slobodkina. il. by author. Reading, Mass.: Addison-Wesley Publishing, 1968.
   Introduce the story: "Let's meet a peddlar who sells caps. What's unusual is that he wears the caps on his head. One day the peddlar decides to take a nap under a tree while keeping his caps on his head. This is the story of what happens during and after the nap."

You will need the following items made of felt: a standing peddlar; a seated peddlar; a set of blue, brown, red, and gray caps; a tree; the sun; and monkeys.

Book Talk

Paddy's New Hat by John S. Goodall. il. by author. New York: Atheneum, 1980.

Introduce the story: "The peddlar in *Caps for Sale* and Olive and Otis in *Olive and the Magic Hat* had problems with hats staying where they're supposed to. In the fingerplay we shared, hats just wouldn't stay on anyone's head. Paddy the pig's new straw hat blows off his head and sets him off into quite an adventure. His journey involves the police, protecting the queen, and catching a thief. But does he get his hat back?"

Who Took the Farmer's Hat? by Joan L. Nodset. il. by Fritz Siebel. New York: Harper & Row, 1963.

Introduce the story: "Like Paddy, the farmer's hat is blown off his head by the wind. He searches and searches and asks the animals on the farm if they've seen his hat. Have any of them seen it—the squirrel, the rabbit, the bird, perhaps?"

Jennie's Hat by Ezra Jack Keats. il. by author. New York: Harper & Row, 1966.

Introduce the story: "Jennie can't wait for the hat to arrive from her aunt. She knows it will be beautiful, flowery, and big. However, when the hat comes it's very different from what Jennie expected. It's just a plain, undecorated hat."

Participation Book

Whose Hat? by Margaret Miller. photographs by author. New York: Greenwillow, 1988.

Introduce the book: "Let's look at the pictures of some hats and see if you can guess who wears them."

The photograph of each hat is followed by a picture of the adult who wears it engaged in a real activity. This is accompanied on the facing page by a photograph of a child wearing the hat engaged in a pretend activity.

Try these hats: fire fighter, police officer, construction worker, and magician.

Participation Book

Whose Hat is That? by Ron Roy. photographs by Rosmarie Hauserr. New York: Clarion Books, 1987.

Introduce the book: "Let's continue our guessing game with this book. There are more hats inside. Let's guess who would wear each type of hat I show you and why they would wear it."

Try the following: swimmer's cap, baseball cap, painter's cap, straw hat, and beekeeper's hat.

TRY THIS!

Read Aloud

Asch, Frank. *Happy Birthday, Moon.* il. by author. Englewood Cliffs, N.J.: Prentice-Hall Books for Young Readers, 1982.

Holland, Isabelle. *Kevin's Hat.* il. by Leonard Lubin. New York: Lothrop, Lee & Shepard Books, 1984.

Johnston, Tony. *The Witch's Hat.* il. by Margot Tomes. New York: Putnam, 1984.

Lear, Edward. *The Quangle Wangle's Hat.* il. by Helen Oxenbury. New York: Franklin Watts, 1970.

Moore, Inga. *Fifty Red Night-Caps.* il. by author. San Francisco, Calif.: Chronicle Books, 1988.

Book Talk

Geringer, Laura. *A Three Hat Day.* il. by Arnold Lobel. New York: Harper & Row, 1985.

Poetry

"The Hat," p. 57 by Karla Kuskin in *Pocket Full of Posies* compiled and written by Gertrude Keyworth. il. by Jerry Ryle and Lorraine Conaway. Flint, Mich.: Flint Public Library, 1984.

Fingerplay and Action Rhyme

"Old John Muddlecombe," p. 14 in *Stamp Your Feet: Action Rhymes* chosen by Sarah Hayes. il. by Toni Goffe. New York: Lothrop, Lee & Shepard Books, 1988.

"What's a hat for?" p. 4 in *Kidstuff*, vol. 4, no. 5, "Hats Off to You" edited by Sheila Debs. Lake Park, Fla.: GuideLines Press, 1986.

Activities

"Soldier's Hat," p. 50 in *Activities for Anyone, Anytime, Anywhere: A Children's Museum Activity Book* by Jeri Robinson. il. by Barbara Bruno. Boston: Little, Brown, 1983.
Demonstrate how to make a four-step hat.

A Place of My Own:
Stories about Houses

PUBLICITY

Create posters and handouts in the shape of a house. Show one large house on your bulletin board with program information appearing behind doors and windows that can be opened. Depict several rooms in a house or show several different silly houses on your board. Use the book *King Boggin's Hall* as your guide. Bibliographic information for this title can be found in the Try This! section of this chapter.

PROGRAM PLAN

Photographs of the inside and outside of your house will intrigue the children. Display the photographs. A dollhouse adds a nice touch. Do you have access to some animal houses such as a fish bowl, a bird house, a cat's basket?

Introduction

Let the children talk about their homes. Direct the discussion by asking questions including: "Do you live in an apartment, a trailer, or a house? Do you have a yard? What color is your home? Do you have your own room or do you share a room with someone? Do you keep your room neat?"

Introduce the program: "People and animals live in all types of homes. Today we're going to share stories about some unusual homes and homes in which unusual things happen."

Poetry

Animal Houses by Aileen Fisher. designed and illustrated by Jan Wills. lettering by Paul Taylor. Glendale, Calif.: Bowmar/Noble Publishers, 1973.

Introduce the poem: "In this poem we'll get to think more about the kinds of houses people and animals live in. Where does a snail live? Do you know where a skunk lives? How about a possum, a mole, or a beaver? Let's find out."

Read Aloud

No Jumping on the Bed by Tedd Arnold. il. by author. New York: Dial Press, 1987.

Introduce the story: "What happens when Walter decides to jump up and down on his bed at night? Could the bed go crashing through the floor with Walter on it? If it did, it would be a wonderful way for Walter to visit and see many different types of rooms in his apartment house."

Fingerplay

"Houses," p. 10 in *Ring a Ring O' Roses: Stories, Games and Finger Plays for Pre-School Children*, rev. ed. Flint, Mich.: Flint Public Library, 1981.

Introduce the fingerplay: "Let's share a story about animal houses."

Try this slowly with the children. Repeat.

Houses

This is a nest for Mr. Bluebird.	(Cup both hands, palms up, little fingers together.)
This is the hive for Mr. Bee.	(Both fists together, palm to palm.)
This is the hole for Bunny Rabbit,	(Make hole, fingertips together.)
And this is the house for me.	(Fingertips together, make a peak.)

Fingerplay

"My House," p. 26 in *Ring a Ring O' Roses: Stories, Games and Finger Plays for Pre-School Children*, rev. ed. Flint, Mich.: Flint Public Library, 1981.
Introduce the fingerplay: "Let's build a house of our own."
Demonstrate. Then invite the children to join you and repeat.

My House

I'm going to build a little house,	(Fingers form roof.)
With windows big and bright.	(Two index fingers and thumbs.)
With chimney tall and curling smoke,	(Stand with arms up in air.)
Drifting out of sight.	
In winter when the snowflakes fall,	(Hands flutter down.)
Or when I hear a storm,	(Hand cupped to ear.)
I'll go sit in my little house,	(Sit down.)
Where I'll be snug and warm.	(Cross arms over chest.)

Read Aloud

Benjy's Dog House by Margaret Bloy Graham. il. by author. New York: Harper & Row, 1973.
Introduce the story: "Benjy the dog is upset. The family has decided that Benjy must sleep outside from now on. Benjy doesn't like his dog house so he decides to find somewhere else to sleep."

Read Aloud

A Blue Seed by Reiko Nakagawa. il. by Yuriko Omura. New York: Hastings House, 1967.
Introduce the story: "Little does Fox know when he trades a blue seed for the boy Yuri's airplane, that Yuri gets the better deal. For when Yuri plants the seed and waters it surprising things happen.

Song

"Go In and Out the Window," p. 47 in *Go In and Out the Window: An Illustrated Songbook for Young People.* music arranged and edited by Dan Fox. commentary by Claude Marks. New York: The Metropolitan Museum of Art/Henry Holt, 1987.

Introduce the song: "Let's share a song called 'Go In and Out the Window.' What do you think the song is about? Are children climbing in and out of a window? Are they sticking their heads in and out of a window?"

Sing the song and then invite the children to join you. Try it faster on the repeat. Try again and have the children lean forward on the word "in" and lean back on the word "out."

This song can also be done as a game at the end of the program. For instructions see: "In and Out the Window," pp. 15-16 in *Party Rhymes* collected and illustrated by Marc Brown. New York: E. P. Dutton, 1988.

Felt-Board Story

"This is the House that Jack Built," pp. 39-43 in *The Flannel Board Storytelling Book* by Judy Sierra. Chicago: H. W. Wilson, 1987.

Introduce the story: "Meet Jack. Jack built a house all by himself. Little did he know what would happen after that."

Instructions and patterns for felt pieces are included with the story.

Book Talk

Alfie Gets in First by Shirley Hughes. il. by author. New York: Lothrop, Lee & Shepard Books, 1981.

Introduce the story: "Alfie races his mom and his sister Annie Rose home. He gets there first. But what he does next gets him into trouble and leads to a parade of neighbors marching to Alfie's house to help."

We Were Tired of Living in a House by Liesel Moak Skorpen. il. by Doris Burn. New York: Coward, McCann & Geoghegan, 1969.

Introduce the story: "If you were tired of living in a house where would you go? Join the children in this story and learn if a tree, a cave, or a pond would make a good home."

The Maid and the Mouse and the Odd-Shaped House, a story in rhyme adapted by Paul O. Zelinsky. New York: Dodd, Mead, 1981.

Introduce the story: "The maid and the mouse are happy in their house until they hear a nasty hissing sound. The maid sets out to discover what is making that odd sound. While she's looking around, the house becomes something very different from what it was."

Activities

"House Sounds Guessing Game" developed by Paula Gaj Sitarz.

Introduce the activity: "Did you ever think about the many sounds you hear in your house every day? Listen to some of the sounds I've recorded in and around my house. Can you tell what made each sound?"

Make a tape of sounds in and around the house. Record each sound for a long period of time so the children will have a chance to identify the sound. Here are some possible sounds to record:

- A clock ticking.
- Water running in a sink or bathtub.
- A telephone ringing (have someone call you on cue).
- A television program (i.e., "Sesame Street," "Mr. Rogers").
- A child laughing.
- A door slamming.
- An alarm clock going off.
- Footsteps.
- An electric shaver.
- A dog barking.
- The buzzer on a microwave.
- A lawn mower.
- A horn blowing on a car.
- A refrigerator humming.
- A can opener.
- A vacuum cleaner.
- A washing machine.
- A doorbell.
- A baby crying.
- A car starting.

TRY THIS!

Read Aloud

Cutler, Ivor. *The Animal House*. il. by Helen Oxenbury. New York: William Morrow, 1977.

Hoberman, Mary Ann. *A House is a House for Me*. il. by Betty Fraser. New York: Viking Press, 1978.

The House that Jack Built. il. by Rodney Peppé. New York: Delacorte Press, 1970.

Miller, Moira. *Oscar Mouse Finds a Home*. il. by Maria Majewska. New York: Dial Books for Young Readers/Dutton, 1985.

Nerlove, Miriam. *I Meant to Clean My Room Today*. il. by author. New York: Margaret K. McElderry Books/Macmillan, 1988.

Peppé, Rodney. *The Mice Who Lived in a Shoe*. il. by author. New York: Lothrop, Lee & Shepard Books, 1981.

Rockwell, Anne, and Harlow Rockwell. *Nice and Clean*. il. by authors. New York: Macmillan, 1984.

Spier, Peter. *Oh, Were They Ever Happy*! il. by author. Garden City, N.Y.: Doubleday, 1978.

Book Talk

Duvoisin, Roger. *The House of Four Seasons*. il. by author. New York: Lothrop, Lee & Shepard Books, 1956.

Geisert, Arthur. *Pigs from A to Z*. il. by author. Boston: Houghton Mifflin, 1986.

Gerstein, Mordecai. *The Room*. il. by author. New York: Harper & Row, 1984.

Hellsing, Lennart. *Wonderful Pumpkin*. il. by Svend Otto. New York: Atheneum, 1976.

Joerns, Consuelo. *The Lost & Found House*. il. by author. New York: Four Winds Press, 1979.

McGovern, Ann. *Mr. Skinner's Skinny House*. il. by Mort Gerberg. New York: Four Winds Press, 1980.

Murphy, Shirley Rousseau. *Tattie's River Journey*. il. by Tomie dePaola. New York: Dial Press, 1983.

Pinkwater, Daniel Manus. *The Big Orange Splot*. il. by author. New York: Hastings House, 1977.

Rockwell, Anne. *The Awful Mess*. il. by author. New York: Four Winds Press, 1973.

Rockwell, Anne, reteller. *Poor Goose: A French Folktale*. il. by Anne Rockwell. New York: Thomas Y. Crowell, 1976.

Other Story Forms

"The House in the Woods," pp. 14-18 and "The Fearsome Beast," pp. 105-111 in *The Flannel Board Storytelling Book* by Judy Sierra. Chicago: H. W. Wilson, 1987.

"The House That Jack Built," pp. 69-80 in *Story Programs: A Source Book of Materials* by Carolyn Sue Peterson and Brenny Hall. Metuchen, N.J.: Scarecrow Press, 1980.

"Peter, Peter Pumpkin Eater," p. 307 in *Handbook for Storytellers* by Carolyn Feller Bauer. Chicago: American Library Association, 1977. (This is a fold-and-cut story.)

Poetry

"The Funny House," pp. 16-17 by Margaret Hillert in *Best Friends* poems selected by Lee Bennett Hopkins. il. by James Watts. New York: Harper & Row, 1986.

"A House is a House for Me," p. 60 by Mary Ann Hoberman in *The Read-Aloud Treasury* compiled by Joanna Cole and Stephanie Calmenson. il. by Ann Schweninger. Garden City, N.Y.: Doubleday, 1988.

"The House Mouse," p. 24 by Jack Prelutsky in *Read-Aloud Rhymes for the Very Young* selected by Jack Prelutsky. il. by Marc Brown. New York: Alfred A. Knopf, 1986.

"Houses," p. 185 by Aileen Fisher in *A New Treasury of Children's Poetry: Old Favorites and New Discoveries* selected and introduced by Joanna Cole. il. by Judith Gwyn Brown. Garden City, N.Y.: Doubleday, 1984. (This poem can be done on the felt board.)

King Boggin's Hall to Nothing-At-All. il. by Blair Lent. Boston: Little, Brown, 1967. (In particular see: "King Boggin's Hall," pp. 2-3, "In a Pumpkin Shell," pp. 10-13, "The Oak," pp. 14-17, "The Old Man in the Kettle," pp. 18-21, and "Under My Hat," pp. 28-29.)

"Tree House," p. 99 by Shel Silverstein in *Sing a Song of Popcorn: Every Child's Book of Poems* selected by Beatrice Schenk de Regniers, Eva Moore, Mary Michaels White, and Jan Carr. il. by nine Caldecott Medal artists. New York: Scholastic, 1988.

"Wanted," p. 37 in *A Child's First Book of Poems*. il. by Cyndy Szekeres. Racine, Wis.: Western Publishing, 1981.

Fingerplay and Action Rhyme

"Different Homes," and "A Good House," p. 19 in *Finger Frolics: Over 250 Fingerplays for Children from 3 Years*, rev. ed. il. by Joan Lockwood. Livonia, Mich.: Partner Press, 1983.

"Here is My Little House," and "I Shut the Door," p. 4 and "Two Cozy Homes," p. 5 in *Kidstuff*, vol. 1, no. 6, "My Home Sweet Home" edited by Sheila Debs. Lake Park, Fla.: GuideLines Press, 1982.

"Two Cozy Homes," p. 22 by Bernice Wells Carlson in *Listen! And Help Tell the Story* by Bernice Wells Carlson. il. by Burmah Burris. Nashville, Tenn.: Abingdon, 1965.

"Two Little Houses," p. 70 and "The House," p. 76 in *Let's Do Fingerplays* by Marion F. Grayson. il. by Nancy Weyl. Washington, D.C.: Robert B. Luce, 1962.

"The Very Nicest Place" adapted as a fingerplay by Paula Gaj Sitarz from an anonymous poem.

The Very Nicest Place

The fish lives in the brook,
(Put two hands together and wiggle.)

The bird lives in the tree,
(Put two arms up as branches.)

But home's the very nicest place
(Form roof with fingertips together.)

For a little child like me.
(Point to self.)

Activities

"Kitchen Ware Guessing Game" developed by Paula Gaj Sitarz.

Set up a screen or a sheet which is illuminated from behind by a lamp. Hold an item found in the kitchen behind the screen and ask the children to guess what it is based on its shadow. Suggested objects include: a large spoon, a fork, a knife, a spatula, a beater, a strainer, a small frying pan, a cookie cutter, a bowl, a place mat, a measuring cup, and a drinking cup.

In the Jungle

You might prefer to be more accurate and call this program "Animals of the Forest and Grassland." Or you might choose to expand the books you can use in this program by naming it "Animals of Other Lands," "Exotic Animals," or "Wild Animals." I prefer "In the Jungle" because it has an air of mystery and and adventure.

PUBLICITY

Provide program information on handouts and posters cut out in the shape of a palm leaf, a safari hat, or a jungle animal. Create a jungle scene on your bulletin board or simply cover it with jungle animals that you draw or cut out from old magazines.

PROGRAM PLAN

Fashion huge palm leaves out of construction paper for your program area or make vines out of green crepe paper. You might like to wear a safari hat and sport a canteen and rope.

Introduction

Introduce the program: "You probably never have visited a real jungle but you can have your own adventure in a jungle with books. Let me show you some of the sights in a jungle."

Book Talk

Junglewalk by Nancy Tafuri. il. by author. New York: Greenwillow, 1988.
Introduce the program: "After the little boy in this book reads about animals who live in the jungle, he see them all in a dream when he goes to sleep at night. There are zebras and tigers, toucans and crocodiles, parrots, elephants, and lions."
Show the corresponding illustrations to give the children an idea of the flora and fauna of a jungle.

Read Aloud

17 Kings and 42 Elephants by Margaret Mahy. il. by Patricia MacCarthy. New York: Dial Books for Young Readers, 1987.
Introduce the story: "Let's join seventeen kings and forty-two elephants as they journey through the jungle on a wild, wet night. What animals will they meet?"

Read Aloud

A Wise Monkey Tale by Betsy and Giulio Maestro. il. by Giulio Maestro. New York: Crown, 1975.
Introduce the story: "Monkey is enjoying a tasty banana cake wrapped in a banana leaf so much that she doesn't see a large hole in front of her and she falls in. Now how will she get out of the hole?"

Fingerplay

"Five Little Monkeys and a Crocodile," in *Going On a Finger Play Hunt* edited
by Cynthia Percak Infantinco. Wheeling, Ill.: Children's Librarians of
North Suburban Library System, 1977. unpaged.
Introduce the fingerplay: "The five monkeys in our next story better
watch out. Here comes a hungry crocodile."
This rhyme has very easy motions that repeat several times. Invite the
children to join you immediately.

Five Little Monkeys and a Crocodile

Five little monkeys swinging in a tree.
(Swing one hand back and forth.)

Along came a crocodile as hungry as can be.
(Make crocodile motions with other hand.)

Snap! went the crocodile.
(Bite one finger with crocodile hand.)

Four little monkeys swinging in a tree.
(Bend down one finger. Repeat above.)

Continue with crocodile bites and verse as above until:

No little monkeys swinging in a tree.
Away went the crocodile as happy as can be!

Read Aloud

The Turtle and the Monkey by Paul Galdone. il. by author. New York: Clarion
Books, 1983.
Introduce the story: "Turtle has found a banana tree floating on the river.
She wants it but she can't get it by herself. Maybe Monkey will help her. I'd
watch out for Monkey, though. He's a tricky fellow."

Book Talk

The Trek by Ann Jonas. il. by author. New York: Greenwillow, 1985.
Introduce the story: "A little girl walks to school every day. It's always an
exciting walk because the little girl goes through a jungle and across a desert.
Do you see those tree trunks? Look carefully. They're really elephants. Those
sacks of garbage? They're rhinoceroses. Those aren't bags of laundry at the
laundromat, they're tropical fish. Those watermelons? A hippopotamus."
You might like to look at this book close-up later. Then you'll be able to
see many other jungle creatures like the peacock, tiger, alligator, and gorillas."

Participation Book

Whose Scaly Tail? by Henrik Drescher. text by Harriet Ziefert. il. by Henrik
Drescher. New York: J. B. Lippincott, 1987.

Introduce the book: "Let's join a young boy as he walks through an African jungle and sees different animals. They're hiding from him. Can you guess what animals they are from the little we can see of them?"

Go slowly and be sure each child has a chance to see and guess which animal is hiding on each page. Try the aardvark, elephant, giraffe, gorilla, and porcupine.

Read Aloud

Where Can an Elephant Hide? by David McPhail. il. by author. Garden City, N.Y.: Doubleday, 1979.

Introduce the story: "Morris the elephant has a problem when he plays hide-and-seek with the other animals in the jungle. He's so huge that he always sticks out from his hiding spot. So what will Morris do? How will he hide when the hunters come toward the jungle animals?"

Book Talk

Crafty Chameleon by Mwenye Hadithi. il. by Adrienne Kennaway. Boston: Little, Brown, 1987.

Introduce the story: "Chameleon has had enough. He's tired of Leopard and Crocodile bothering and menacing him. How can he make them stop? Chameleon thinks of a clever trick. The most wonderful part of his plan is that Leopard and Crocodile will never know that Chameleon had anything to do with what happens to them."

Greedy Zebra by Mwenye Hadithi. il. by Adrienne Kennaway. Boston: Little, Brown, 1984.

Introduce the story: "Do you know why Zebra has black and white stripes? It began when the world was new. Zebra wouldn't stop eating grass long enough to see what wonderful things were in the mysterious cave. There were animal skins, beautiful colors, and other body features. By the time Zebra visited the cave nothing was left."

Hot Hippo by Mwenye Hadithi. il. by Adrienne Kennaway. Boston: Little, Brown, 1986.

Introduce the story: "Hippo is so hot and unhappy living on the dry land. He wants to swim in the water. But Ngai says Hippo can't swim in the water. Ngai is afraid that Hippo will eat all the fish. Can Hippo change Ngai's mind?"

Creative Dramatics

"Jungle Animals" developed by Paula Gaj Sitarz.

Introduce the activity: "Let's pretend to be some of the jungle animals we've met today."

Be sure you have enough space for this activity. State what animal you're going to be then let the children interpret the animal's behavior any way they wish. Then show the children your interpretation and let them imitate you if they wish.

Suggested animals and their activities:

- Hippopotamus in a muddy pool of water lumbering about and opening its big mouth to eat fish.

- Monkey climbing a tree and eating bananas.

- A slow moving tortoise looking from side to side.

- Python slithering and sticking its tongue out.

- A roaring lion.

- A cheetah, jaguar, or gazelle running swiftly and leaping.

- A lizard or iguana catching flies with its tongue.

- A giraffe reaching with its long neck to eat leaves off a tree.

- A hyena laughing.

- An elephant swinging his trunk and spraying himself with water.

TRY THIS!

Read Aloud

Aitken, Amy. *Kate and Moira in the Jungle.* il. by author. Scarsdale, N.Y.: Bradbury Press, 1981.

Aruego, Jose, and Ariane Dewey. *A Crocodile's Tale: A Philippine Folk Story.* il. by authors. New York: Scribner's, 1972.

Aruego, Jose, and Ariane Dewey. *Rockabye Crocodile.* il. by authors. New York: Greenwillow, 1988.

Brenner, Barbara. *Mr. Tall and Mr. Small.* il. by Tomi Ungerer. Reading, Mass.: Addison-Wesley Publishing, 1966.

Harper, Wilhelmina. *The Gunniwolf.* il. by William Wiesner. New York: E. P. Dutton, 1967. (This adapts well as a felt-board story.)

Higham, Jon Atlas. *Aardvark's Picnic.* il. by author. Boston: Little, Brown, 1986.

Kimmel, Eric A., reteller. *Anansi and the Moss-Covered Rock.* il. by Janet Stevens. New York: Holiday House, 1988.

Kishida, Eriko. *The Lion and the Bird's Nest.* il. by Chiyoko Nakatani. New York: Thomas Y. Crowell, 1973.

Maestro, Giulio, reteller. *The Tortoise's Tug of War.* il. by author. Scarsdale, N.Y.: Bradbury Press, 1971.

Thaler, Mike. *Moonkey.* il. by Guilio Maestro. New York: Harper & Row, 1981.

Troughton, Joanna. *Tortoise's Dream*. il. by author. New York: Peter Bedrick Books, 1986.

Wildsmith, Brian. *Python's Party*. il. by author. New York: Franklin Watts, 1975.

Book Talk

Aruego, Jose and Ariane Dewey. *We Hide, You Seek*. il. by authors. New York: Greenwillow, 1979.

Dee, Ruby, reteller. *Two Ways to Count to Ten: A Liberian Folktale*. il. by Susan Meddaugh. New York: Henry Holt, 1988.

Demarest, Chris L. *No Peas for Nellie*. il. by author. New York: Macmillan, 1988.

Sis, Peter. *Rainbow Rhino*. il. by author. New York: Alfred A. Knopf, 1987.

Other Story Forms

"The Elephant's Child," pp. 10-24 adapted by Becky Pearce in *Kidstuff*, vol. 3, no. 4, "Elephants-Smellaphants" edited by Sheila Debs. Lake Park, Fla.: GuideLines Press, 1984. (This is a felt-board story.)

"The Fearsome Beast," pp. 105-111 and "Uwungelema," pp. 152-157 in *The Flannel Board Storytelling Book* by Judy Sierra. Chicago: H. W. Wilson, 1987.

Poetry

"Hippopotamus," p. 95 by Joanna Cole in *A New Treasury of Children's Poetry: Old Favorites and New Discoveries* selected and introduced by Joanna Cole. il. by Judith Gwyn Brown. Garden City, N.Y.: Doubleday, 1984.

Fingerplay and Action Rhyme

"The Alligator," p. 32 in *Let's Do Fingerplays* by Marion F. Grayson. il. Nancy Weyl. Washington, D.C.: Robert B. Luce, 1962.

"The Crocodile," p. 15 in *Play Rhymes* collected by Marc Brown. il. by author. New York: E. P. Dutton, 1987.

"An Elephant Goes Like This and That," p. 103 in *Games for the Very Young: Finger Plays and Nursery Games* compiled by Elizabeth Matterson. New York: American Heritage Press/McGraw Hill, 1971.

"The Elephant's Trunk" and "Five Gray Elephants," p. 79 in *Finger Frolics: Over 250 Fingerplays for Children from 3 Years*, rev. ed. compiled by Liz Cromwell, Dixie Hibner, and John R. Faitel. il. by Joan Lockwood. Livonia, Mich.: Partner Press, 1983.

"The Giraffe," p. 4 in *Kidstuff*, vol. 1, no. 2, "Razzle Dazzle Circus" edited by Sheila Debs. Lake Park, Fla.: GuideLines Press, 1981.

"Mr. Lion," p. 4 in *Kidstuff*, vol. 3, no. 8, "Lots of Lions," edited by Sheila Debs. Lake Park, Fla.: GuideLines Press, 1985.

"Three Little Monkeys," p. 15 in *Clap Your Hands: Finger Rhymes* chosen by Sarah Hayes. il. by Toni Goffe. New York: Lothrop, Lee & Shepard Books, 1988.

Activities

"Jungle Animal Guessing Game" developed by Paula Gaj Sitarz.
Give the children clues about various jungle animals and let them guess which animals you are talking about. Try these clues:

- I enjoy swinging from trees and sometimes I hang from them by my tail. If you give me a banana to eat I'll be your friend.   (monkey)

- I am huge and gray and most people think I'm afraid of mice. I know I have an enormous nose. Would you like a ride on it?   (elephant)

- I have a large mouth with rows of strong sharp teeth. You can find me living in the water swishing my powerful green tail. (alligator/crocodile)

- Am I black with white stripes or white with black stripes? I look something like a horse but you know what I really am.   (zebra)

- I am the king of the jungle. I have a full crop of hair on my face and head which people call a mane. Have you ever heard me roar?   (lion)

- I am also a large cat like the lion. But I have orange and black stripes. I am also a very fast runner.   (tiger)

- I am long and I slither along the ground because I have no arms or legs. I can even shed my skin.   (snake)

- I am tall and my neck is very long. My neck allows me to reach leaves in the tree tops. I like to munch on them.   (giraffe)

- I'm gray and I like to wallow in a muddy pool of water. When I open my huge mouth you can see my enormous teeth. (hippopotamus)

To the Moon

PUBLICITY

A full or crescent moon or a space shuttle are possible shapes for your handouts and posters. Create a moon mobile on which you can provide information about the program. Tack photographs of the moon, perhaps in all its phases, on a bulletin board. Show photographs of the space shuttle orbiting the moon and the lunar rover on the moon.

PROGRAM PLAN

Decorate the program area by suspending a paper moon, planets, and stars from the ceiling. Perhaps you have a globe of the moon to display?

Introduction

Introduce the program: "Do you ever look up at the moon in the evening? It's always changing, isn't it? Sometimes it seems as round and bright as the sun. Other times it looks like a small sliver. Sometimes the moon is hidden by clouds and sometimes you can see the moon during the day. In the stories we share today, we'll see the moon in different ways too and we'll find out how the moon can cause problems for people and animals."

Read Aloud

The Boy in the Moon by Ib Spang Olsen. translated from the Danish by Virginia Allen Jensen. il. by author. New York: Parents Magazine Press, 1977.

Introduce the story: "The boy in the moon is sent on quite an adventure. The man in the moon sees his reflection in the water on earth. He thinks that his reflection is another moon and he sends the boy in the moon to get it for him. There are dangers on the way down. And, what will the boy in the moon discover once he gets to earth?"

Fingerplay

"Moon Ride," p. 73 in *Ring a Ring O' Roses: Stories, Games and Finger Plays for Pre-School Children*, rev. ed., Flint, Mich.: Flint Public Library, 1981.

Introduce the fingerplay: "Other people have been on the moon and now it's time for us to get in a rocket ship and blast off."

The children will want to do this with you right away. And, they will certainly want to repeat it.

Moon Ride

Do you want to go up with me to the moon?	(Point to friend, self, then to sky.)
Let's get in our rocket ship and blast off soon!	(Pretend to climb in ship.)
Faster and faster we reach to the sky.	(Swish hands quickly.) (Jump and reach.)
Isn't it fun to be able to fly?	
We're on the moon, now all take a look.	(Look down.)
And gently sit down and I'll show you a book.	(Sit down gently.)

Read Aloud

Squawk to the Moon, Little Goose by Edna Mitchell Preston. il. by Barbara Cooney. New York: Viking Press, 1974.

Introduce the story: "No sooner is Mother Goose out the door, than Little Goose heads for the pond. On the way, guess what Little Goose sees in the sky. The moon swallowed by a white fox. Can that be?"

Read Aloud

Moongame by Frank Asch. il. by author. Englewood Cliffs, N.J.: Prentice-Hall, 1984.

Introduce the story: "Bear has learned how to play hide-and-seek with Bird and now he wants to play the game with the moon. The game doesn't turn out the way Bear expected."

Book Talk

Moon Bear by Frank Asch. il. by author. New York: Scribner's 1978.

Introduce the story: "Poor Moon Bear! He's so worried about the moon. It seems to get thinner and thinner every night. Maybe it will disappear completely. If Moon Bear leaves food for the moon, maybe it will fatten up and get bigger and rounder."

Song

"Aikendrum," p. 7 in *The Raffi Singable Songbook: A Collection of 51 Songs from Raffi's First Three Records for Young Children*. il. by Joyce Yamamoto. New York: Crown, 1987.

Introduce the song: "Did you know that there was a man who lived on the moon? His name was Aikendrum and he had some unusual features, at least according to this song."

This is a simple song to learn. The children will enjoy singing all the verses.

Felt-Board Story

Why the Sun and the Moon Live in the Sky: An African Folktale by Elphinstone Dayrell. il. by Blair Lent. Boston: Houghton Mifflin, 1968.

Introduce the story: "According to this story the sun and the moon didn't
always live in the sky. They lived on the earth. But one day the water came to
visit the sun and the moon and this is what happened."

You will need the following items made of felt: sun, water, water's house,
moon, frame of sun's new house, sun's new house, and the fish and water
animals.

Action Rhyme

"Ring Around the Rocket Ship," p. 35 in *Ring a Ring O' Roses: Stories, Games
and Finger Plays for Pre-School Children*, rev. ed. Flint, Mich.: Flint
Public Library, 1981.

Introduce the fingerplay: "Now that we've talked about the moon, the
sun, and space, let's take another trip in a rocket ship. This time instead of
blasting off to the moon let's aim for the stars."

Do this slowly with the children and then try it faster.

Ring Around the Rocket Ship

Ring around the rocket ship.	(All join hands in circle and walk to the right.)
Try to grab a star.	(At the word "grab", drop hands and reach up.)
Stardust, stardust Fall where you are.	(On the word "fall", fall to the floor.)

Activities

"Moon Cookies," p. 334 in *Handbook for Storytellers* by Caroline Feller
Bauer. Chicago: American Library Association, 1977.

This is an easy no-cook recipe to share with a group. The ingredients
include peanut butter, honey, wheat germ, dried milk, and graham cracker
crumbs. Invite the children to help pour the ingredients into a bowl and to then
take turns mixing them. Give each child enough dough to form individual balls
or "moons". Let the children roll their "moons" in powdered sugar. The
children can eat their "moons" at the program or bring them home to enjoy
later.

TRY THIS!

Read Aloud

Asch, Frank. *Happy Birthday, Moon*. il. by author. Englewood Cliffs, N.J.:
Prentice-Hall, 1982.

Asch, Frank. *Starbaby*. il. by author. New York: Scribner's, 1980.

Brown, Margaret Wise. *Goodnight Moon*. il. by author. New York: Harper & Row, 1947.

Holl, Adelaide. *Moon Mouse*. il. by Cyndy Szekeres. New York: Random House, 1969.

Thaler, Mike. *Moonkey*. il. by Giulio Maestro. New York: Harper & Row, 1981.

Book Talk

Alexander, Martha. *Maggie's Moon*. il. by author. New York: Dial Press, 1982.

Carle, Eric. *Papa, Please Get the Moon for Me*. il. by author. Saxonville, Mass.: Picture Book Studio, 1986.

Chorao, Kay. *Lemon Moon*. il. by author. New York: Holiday House, 1983.

Levitin, Sonia. *Who Owns the Moon?* il. by John Larrecq. Berkeley, Calif.: Parnassus Press, 1973.

Udry, Janice May. *The Moon Jumpers*. il. by Maurice Sendak. New York: Harper & Row, 1959.

Poetry

"The Star," p. 71 by Jane Taylor in *Read-Aloud Rhymes for the Very Young* selected by Jack Prelutsky. il. by Marc Brown. New York: Alfred A. Knopf, 1986. (This can be done as a fingerplay.)

"Winter Moon," p. 48 by Langston Hughes in *The Random House Book of Poetry for Children: A Treasury of 572 Poems for Today's Child* selected by Jack Prelutsky. il. by Arnold Lobel. New York: Random House, 1983.

Fingerplay and Action Rhyme

"Johnny's Ride," p. 23 and "Space Rocket," p. 53 in *Listen! And Help Tell the Story* by Bernice Wells Carlson. il. by Burmah Burris. Nashville, Tenn.: Abingdon, 1965.

Song

"Twinkle, Twinkle, Little Star," p. 64 in *Singing Bee! A Collection of Favorite Children's Songs* compiled by Jane Hart. il. by Anita Lobel. New York: Lothrop, Lee & Shepard Books, 1982.

Film

Why the Sun and the Moon Live in the Sky. Glendale, Calif.: AIMS Instructional Media, Inc., 1970. 11 min.

Let's Have a Party!

This program consists of stories about parties other than those given for birthdays or in honor of holidays. For stories about those parties see my book *Picture Book Story Hours: From Birthdays to Bears* (Libraries Unlimited, 1987) and the chapters "Goblins and Ghosts: Halloween Stories," "Happy Birthday to You!" and "Seasons Greetings: Christmas Stories."

PUBLICITY

Make handouts and posters in the shape of a gift package, a party hat, or an invitation. Lift the flap on the "poster invitation" to reveal information about the program. Do the same on your bulletin board or decorate it with items associated with parties.

PROGRAM PLAN

A few balloons, streamers, and party hats in the program area will create a festive atmosphere. Wear a special outfit for the occasion.

Introduction

Introduce the program: "People have parties for lots of reasons. There are parties to celebrate holidays like Christmas, Halloween, Valentine's Day, and the Fourth of July. Birthday parties are always fun. But people also have parties to get together with friends, to dress in costumes, or to celebrate a season. We'll meet many party goers in the stories we share today. They're going to all types of parties."

Read Aloud

Dandelion by Don Freeman. il. by author. New York: Viking Press, 1964.
    Introduce the story: "Dandelion is so excited. He's been invited to a party at Miss Giraffe's house. There'll be friends to see and goodies to eat. Dandelion must get ready. I wonder if he'll have a good time at the party?"

Book Talk

Portly McSwine by James Marshall. il. by author. Boston: Houghton Mifflin, 1979.
    Introduce the story: "Portly McSwine is a funny fellow. He's giving a big party and he's never given one, and he's so worried. What if he's sick for the party? He runs to the doctor's for a flu shot. What if his guests don't think he's funny enough? So Portly practices telling jokes. Portly worries that his food won't be tasty and his dancing will be terrible. Poor Portly. And, when his party is a big success, what do you think Portly worries about?"

Book Talk

Python's Party by Brian Wildsmith. il. by author. New York: Franklin Watts, 1975.

Introduce the story: Meet Python, a large snake who lives in the jungle. He's hungry and wants some animals to eat. The animals always hide from Python because they don't want to be eaten by him. One day Python is so hungry that he calls the animals together and invites them to a party. He promises he'll be good so all the animals agree to come. But Python has a trick planned for his party. Hyena, Fox, Pelican, Elephant, and all the other animals better watch out."

Fingerplay

"Party Time" by Paula Gaj Sitarz.

Introduce the fingerplay: "Let's join some children who are enjoying a party."

There are many actions in this rhyme so demonstrate first. Then invite the children to join you. Repeat.

Party Time

Streamers hang everywhere.
(Spiral motion with right hand.)

Balloons float in the air.
(Form circle with hands. Float in air.)

Sue and Max eat their cake.
(Imitate eating cake.)

Someone laughs hard, it's Jake
(Hold stomach and pretend to laugh.)

Tim pins the tail on the donkey.
(Pretend to pin tail.)

Jill plays a record with Tony.
(Twirl index finger on right hand.)

What is everyone doing? What is the fuss?
(Arms out wide.)

We're having a great party.
(Throw arms in air.)

Come and join us.
(Arms outstretched in welcome.)

Read Aloud

Annie and the Mud Monster by Dick Gackenbach. il. by author. New York: Lothrop, Lee & Shepard Books, 1982.

Introduce the story: "Annie is off to a costume party dressed as a potato. You see, everyone is supposed to dress like a vegetable for this party. But something doesn't seem right with Annie's costume. Someone or something agrees with her. Can *it* help Annie with the problem?"

Read Aloud

The Surprise Party by Pat Hutchins. il. by author. New York: Macmillan, 1969.

Introduce the story: "Rabbit is planning a party. He tells Owl that it's a surprise. Owl tells Squirrel, anyway. He gets the information wrong, however, and tells Squirrel that Rabbit is doing something very different from what he said. As Squirrel and all the other animals pass the secret, the information gets stranger and stranger. Everyone has a different idea of what Rabbit is planning."

Song

"The More We Get Together," pp. 52-53 in *The Raffi Singable Songbook: A Collection of 51 Songs from Raffi's First Three Records for Young Children.* il. by Joyce Yamamoto. New York: Crown, 1987.

Introduce the song: "One important reason for having a party is to be with people—people we know and people we'd like to know. Let's sing a song about getting together."

This is an easy tune that some of the children may know. Sing it several times until everyone is comfortable with the song.

Read Aloud

Spring Green by Valrie H. Selkowe. il. by Jeni Crisler Barrett. New York: Lothrop, Lee & Shepard Books, 1985.

Introduce the story: "What is Danny Duck going to do? He needs something for the "green" contest at the spring party. All the other animals have something green to take, but not Danny. Or does he?"

Activities

"Party Items Memory Game" developed by Paula Gaj Sitarz.

Do ahead: Collect items associated with parties and place them on a tray. These can include: party hat, balloon, present, candle, napkin, invitation, roll of crepe paper, streamers, horn, cookies, flowers, card, a cassette or record. If you prefer, fashion the items out of felt and add: a cup of juice, cake, clown, ice cream cone, and a child in a party outfit. Put the felt items on a felt board.

During the program: Ask the children to look at the items on the tray or on the felt board. Cover the tray or felt board and remove one item. Remove the cover and ask the children which item you removed. Try this activity several times removing a different object each time.

TRY THIS!

Read Aloud

Allard, Harry. *There's a Party at Mona's Tonight.* il. by James Marshall. Garden City, N.Y.: Doubleday, 1981.

Brandenberg, Franz. *The Hit of the Party*. il. by Aliki. New York: Greenwillow, 1985.

De Regniers, Beatrice Schenk. *May I Bring a Friend?* il. by Beni Montresor. New York: Atheneum, 1982.

Lobel, Anita. *The Troll Music*. il. by author. New York: Harper & Row, 1966.

Sharmat, Marjorie Weinman. *The 329th Friend*. il. by Cyndy Szekeres. New York: Four Winds Press, 1979.

Book Talk

Bollinger, Max. *The Giant's Feast*. il. by Monica Laimgruber. Reading, Mass.: Addison-Wesley, 1976.

Cohen, Miriam. *Tough Jim*. il. by Lillian Hoban. New York: Macmillan, 1974.

Freeman, Don. *The Paper Party*. il. by author. New York: Viking Press, 1974.

Hughes, Shirley. *Alfie Gives a Hand*. il. by author. New York: Lothrop, Lee & Shepard Books, 1983.

Activities

Brown, Marc, collector. *Party Rhymes*. il. by Marc Brown. New York: E. P. Dutton, 1988.

"The Hokey-Pokey," p. 19 in *Wee Sing and Play: Musical Games and Rhymes for Children* by Pamela Conn Beall and Susan Hagen Nipp. il. by Nancy Klein. Los Angeles: Price/Stern/Sloan Publishing, 1986.

All about Pets

PUBLICITY

Draw paw prints on your handouts and posters or create them in the shape of a doghouse, cat's basket, bird cage, dog bone, turtle, hamster, or mouse. Cut out and tack pictures of animals that make good pets on a bulletin board. Or, be more imaginative and cut items out of construction paper that you associate with pets like a dog bone, a hamster's cage, or a cat's toy and put them on your board as well.

PROGRAM PLAN

Stuffed toy animals including dogs, cats, mice, rabbits, and birds will make your program area eye appealing. Bring in a quiet pet like a turtle or fish that won't be distracting.

Introduction

Encourage the children to talk about their pets or the pets they'd like to have some day.

Poetry

"Cats and Dogs," by N. M. Bodecker and "Hamsters," by Marci Ridlon, p. 54
in *Read-Aloud Rhymes for the Very Young* selected by Jack Prelutsky. il.
by Marc Brown. New York: Alfred A. Knopf, 1986.
Introduce the poems: "You might think that cats and dogs make the best pets, but listen to the children in these poems. They have other ideas about what animals make the best pets. See of you agree."
Be sure to share the illustrations from the book with the children as you read the poems.

Read Aloud

Dog for a Day by Dick Gackenbach. il. by author. New York: Clarion Books,
1987.
Introduce the story: "Sydney creates so many problems at home with his invention that changes things. He turns a football into a toaster. He turns the baby into a lamp. What would happen if Sydney turned his pet dog Wally into him and himself into Wally? Would it work or would there be problems?"

Tell and Draw Story

"Choosing a Pet," pp. 20-21 in *Tell and Draw Stories* by Margaret J. Olson.
Minneapolis, Minn.: Creative Storytime Press, 1963.
Introduce the story: "Mary and David are so excited. They've been given permission to go to the pet shop to buy a pet. Let's join them as they walk around the store and try to choose a pet. Which pet would you pick?"

Fingerplay

"My Pets," p. 19 in *Ring a Ring O' Roses: Stories, Games and Finger Plays for Pre-School Children*, rev. ed. Flint, Mich.: Flint Public Library, 1981.

Introduce the fingerplay: "What would it be like to own and care for five pets? Let's meet the young person who owns them and find out."

This is an easy counting rhyme so have the children join you immediately. Repeat.

My Pets

I have five pets (Hold up five fingers.)
That I'd like you to meet. Starting with the little finger,
They all live on Mulberry Street. point to each as verse
This is my chicken, progresses.)
The smallest of all.
He comes running whenever
    I call.
This is my duckling.
He says: "Quack, quack, quack,"
As he shakes the water from
    his back.
Here is my rabbit, he runs from
    his pen.
Then I must put him back again.
This is my kitten.
Her coat is black and white.
She loves to sleep on my pillow
    at night.
Here is my puppy who has lots
    of fun.
He chases the others and makes (Move thumb slowly and
    them run. fingers rapidly.)

Read Aloud

Annie and the Wild Animals by Jan Brett. il. by author. Boston: Houghton Mifflin, 1985.

Introduce the story: "Annie's pet cat Taffy is acting strange. Taffy doesn't want to be with Annie and Annie is lonely. Annie has an idea, though. If she leaves corn cakes outside on the ground maybe an animal will come and Annie can keep it as a pet."

Book Talk

Hemi's Pet by Joan de Hamel. il. by Christine Ross. Boston: Houghton Mifflin, 1987.

Introduce the story: "Hemi's class is going to have a pet show but Hemi is sad because he doesn't have a pet. What will he do? His sister Rata has an idea. I wonder if it will help."

Emma's Pet by David McPhail. il. by author. New York: E. P. Dutton, 1985.
Introduce the story: "Like Annie and Hemi, Emma is looking for the perfect pet. It should be warm, soft, and cuddly. All the animals she meets just aren't right. Will *she* ever have a pet?"

Song

"Where, Oh Where Has My Little Dog Gone?" p. 113 in *Singing Bee! A Collection of Favorite Children's Songs* compiled by Jane Hart. il. by Anita Lobel. New York: Lothrop, Lee & Shepard Books, 1982.
Introduce the song: "How would you feel if you lost your pet? Let's join the young person who is singing this song about his lost dog."
Enjoy this short song with the children several times.

Read Aloud

Six Dogs, Twenty-Three Cats, Forty-Five Mice, and One Hundred Sixteen Spiders by Mary Chalmers. il. by author. New York: Harper & Row, 1986.
Introduce the story: "Annie Tree lives in a little yellow house with 190 pets. She loves her pets but her friend Priscilla doesn't care for them that much. What can Annie do? How can she keep her pets and her friend?"

Book Talk

Parakeets and Peach Pies by Kay Smith. il. by Jose Aruego. New York: Parents Magazine Press, 1970.
Introduce the story: "Matthew wants to ask his mom a question but first she has something to show him. It's about his many pets including a parakeet, lizard, snake, cat, dog, frog, and fish. Now how will Matthew ask his question—if he can get another pet?"

Book Talk

Pet Show! by Ezra Jack Keats. il. by author. New York: Macmillan, 1972.
Introduce the story: "Poor Archie! All the kids are on their way to the neighborhood pet show and Archie's cat has disappeared. Now Archie has no pet to enter in the show. What will he do?"

Film

The Mongrel Dog. New York: McGraw-Hill Films, 1972. 6 min.
Introduce the film: "Let's watch a little girl who has entered her dogs in a show. All of them perform their tricks very well, except one. What will happen to that dog?"

TRY THIS!

Read Aloud

Batherman, Muriel. *Some Things You Should Know About My Dog*. il. by author. Englewood Cliffs, N.J.: Prentice-Hall, 1976.

Brandenberg, Franz. *Aunt Nina's Visit*. il. by Aliki. New York: Greenwillow, 1984.

Brandenberg, Franz. *The Hit of the Party*. il. by Aliki. New York: Greenwillow, 1985.

Brown, Ruth. *Our Cat Flossie*. il. by author. New York: E. P. Dutton, 1986.

Brown, Ruth. *Our Puppy's Vacation*. il. by author. New York: E. P. Dutton, 1987.

Cuyler, Margery. *Freckles and Willie*. il. by Marsha Winborn. New York: Holt, Rinehart and Winston, 1986.

Gackenbach, Dick. *A Bag Full of Pups*. il. by author. Boston: Ticknor & Fields/Houghton Mifflin, 1981.

Gantos, Jack. *Rotten Ralph*. il. by Nicole Rubel. Boston: Houghton Mifflin, 1976.

Keats, Ezra Jack. *Whistle for Willie*. il. by author. New York: Viking Press, 1964.

Kellogg, Steven. *Can I Keep Him?* il. by author. New York: Dial Press, 1971.

Kellogg, Steven. *The Mysterious Tadpole*. il. by author. New York: Dial Press, 1977.

Kudrna, Charlene Imbior. *To Bathe a Boa*. il. by author. Minneapolis, Minn.: Carolrhoda Books, 1986.

McPhail, David. *Great Cat*. il. by author. New York: E. P. Dutton, 1982.

Old Mother Hubbard and Her Dog. il. by Evaline Ness. New York: Holt, Rinehart and Winston, 1972.

Parker, Nancy Winslow. *Love From Uncle Clyde*. il. by author. New York: Dodd, Mead, 1977.

Peterson, Esther Allen. *Frederick's Alligator*. il. by Susanna Natti. New York: Crown, 1979.

Schwartz, Amy. *Oma and Bobo*. il. by author. Scarsdale, N.Y.: Bradbury Press, 1987.

Ungerer, Tomi. *Crictor*. il. by author. New York: Harper & Row, 1958.

Wildsmith, Brian. *Pelican*. il. by author. New York: Pantheon, 1982.

Zion, Gene. *Harry the Dirty Dog*. il. by Margaret Bloy Graham. New York: Harper & Row, 1956

Book Talk

Barton, Byron. *Jack and Fred*. il. by author. New York: Macmillan, 1974.

Gag, Wanda. *Millions of Cats*. il. by author. New York: Coward, McCann & Geoghegan, 1928.

Kellogg, Steven. *A Rose for Pinkerton*. il. by author. New York: Dial Press, 1981.

Lindgren, Barbro. *The Wild Baby Gets a Puppy*. il. by Eva Eriksson. adapted from the Swedish by Jack Prelutsky. New York: Greenwillow, 1985, 1988.

Morgan, Michaela. *Edward Gets a Pet*. il. by Sue Porter. New York: E. P. Dutton, 1987.

Noble, Trinka H. *The Day Jimmy's Boa Ate the Wash*. il. by author. New York: Dial Press, 1980.

Parker, Nancy Winslow. *Poofy Loves Company*. il. by author. New York: Dodd, Mead, 1980.

Samuels, Barbara. *Duncan & Dolores*. il. by author. Scarsdale, N.Y.: Bradbury Press, 1986.

Poetry

"Cats," p. 68 by Eleanor Farjeon in *The Random House Book of Poetry for Children: A Treasury of 572 Poems for Today's Child* selected by Jack Prelutsky. il. by Arnold Lobel. New York: Random House, 1983.

"The House Cat," p. 18 by Annette Wynne and "Chums," p. 40 by Arthur Guiterman in *Read-Aloud Rhymes for the Very Young* selected by Jack Prelutsky. il. by Marc Brown. New York: Alfred A. Knopf, 1986.

"My Cat, Mrs. Lick-a-Chin," p. 66 by John Ciardi in *Sing a Song of Popcorn: Every Child's Book of Poems* selected by Beatrice Schenk de Regniers, Eva Moore, Mary Michaels White, and Jan Carr. il. by nine Caldecott Medal artists. New York: Scholastic, 1988.

"My Puppy," p. 20 in *A Child's First Book of Poems*. il. by Cyndy Szekeres. Racine, Wis.: Western Publishing, 1981.

"Spelling Lesson," p. 64 by Stephanie Calmenson in *The Read-Aloud Treasury* compiled by Joanna Cole and Stephanie Calmenson. il. by Ann Schweninger. Garden City, N.Y.: Doubleday, 1988.

Fingerplay and Action Rhyme

"Animals," p. 25 in *Play Rhymes* collected by Marc Brown. il. by author. New York: E. P. Dutton, 1987.

"Poor Dog, Poor Mo," p. 56 in *Listen! And Help Tell the Story* by Beatrice Wells Carlson. il. by Burmah Burris. Nashville, Tenn.: Abingdon, 1965.

Song

"BINGO," p. 13 in *Eye Winker, Tom Tinker, Chin Chopper* by Tom Glazer. il. by Ron Himler. Garden City, N.Y.: Doubleday, 1973.

Filmstrip

Hi, Cat! New York: Macmillan Library Services, 1974. 3 min. 30 sec.

Pet Show! New York: Macmillan Library Services, 1974. 4 min. 35 sec.

Film

Lend a Paw. Burbank, Calif.: Walt Disney Company, 1941. 8 min.

Let's Go on a Picnic

PUBLICITY

Border your handouts and posters with ants. Or, design handouts in the shape of a folded napkin and create posters in the shape of a picnic basket. Lift the lid on the basket to reveal information about the program. Your bulletin board becomes a picnic basket full of sandwiches, cookies, plates, napkins, and juice. If you prefer, create a picnic scene on your board.

PROGRAM PLAN

Let the children sit on a blanket or a red-and-white-check tablecloth. Pull books used in the program from a picnic basket.

Introduction

Introduce the program: "Have you ever been on a picnic? They're lots of fun, whether you're at a park, a pond, the beach, in your backyard, or in a forest. There are games to play. Maybe you'll go swimming or play baseball. You might row a boat, fish, or enjoy the swings and slides. Whatever you do and wherever you go, you'll soon be hungry and it will be time to eat. You'll enjoy sandwiches, cookies, juice or lemonade, and maybe a delicious watermelon.

Sometimes, though, people have troubles on their picnics as we'll see in some of the stories we share today."

Read Aloud

The Bear's Water Picnic by John Yeoman. il. by Quentin Blake. New York: Atheneum, 1987.

Introduce the story: "Poor Bear, Pig, Hen, Squirrel, and Hedgehog. A group of frogs ruin their lovely picnic. But, when the animal friends run into trouble, guess who helps them?"

Fingerplay

"Picnic in the Park" by Paula Gaj Sitarz.

Introduce the fingerplay: "Join my friends and me on our picnic in the park."

Demonstrate this finger rhyme while the children watch and listen. Invite the children to join you and then repeat.

Picnic in the Park

We packed sandwiches, cookies and juice,
(Pretend to pack.)

And went for a walk to the park.
(Walk index and middle fingers of right hand.)

We found a tree with lots of shade,
(Arms up in air to form branches of tree.)

And spread our blanket beneath.
(Pretend to spread blanket.)

But what do you think happened,
(Shrug shoulders.)

When we started to eat our food?
One squirrel scampered over —
(Hold up one finger.)

Two birds chirped close by —
(Hold up two fingers.)

And hundreds of ants marched up to us,
(Flash ten fingers several times.)

All to share our food.
(Pretend to pass out food.)

Read Aloud

Aardvark's Picnic by Jon Atlas Higham. il. by author. Boston, Mass.: Little, Brown, 1986.

Introduce the story: "Aardvark is so upset. He's supposed to provide ants for the picnic. His friends will be disappointed if they can't enjoy ant salad and chocolate ant rolls. Where could he have put the ants? As Aardvark heads for the picnic spot he asks the other animals if they have any ants. Let's see if they do."

Song

"The Ants Came Marching," pp. 82-83 in *Sally Go Round the Sun: 300 Children's Songs, Rhymes and Games* collected and edited by Edith Fowke. il. by Carlos Marchiori. Garden City, N.Y.: Doubleday, 1969.

Introduce the song: "Ants! They seem to turn up at picnics everywhere. Let's sing this song about an army of ants, pretending that they're marching toward someone's picnic."

This is a long and repetitive song so invite the children to join you at any point. Sing the song through or stop after several verses if interest wanes.

Read Aloud

The Pigs' Picnic by Keiko Kasza. il. by author. New York: Putnam, 1988.

Introduce the story: "Mr. Pig is on his way to Miss Pig's house to invite her on a picnic. On the way Fox, Lion, and Zebra each give Mr. Pig something to make him look more handsome. What will Miss Pig think when she sees Mr. Pig? Will she want to go on a picnic with him?"

Read Aloud

Winter Picnic by Robert Welber. il. by Deborah Ray. New York: Pantheon, 1970.

Introduce the story: "You probably think that people only enjoy picnics in the spring, summer, and fall. But what about a picnic in the winter? Would you enjoy that? Adam wants to have an outdoor picnic in the snow but his mother isn't sure about the idea."

Fingerplay

"A Picnic" by Paula Gaj Sitarz.
Introduce the fingerplay: "Let's talk about the different places where you can have a picnic."
There are several motions in this finger rhyme so demonstrate first and then have the children join you. If they seem interested, repeat.

A Picnic

In the park
(Arms up to form branches of tree.)

Or at the beach
(Swimming motions.)

In a boat
(Rowing motions.)

Or hiking.
(Stamp feet.)

A picnic is fun
Wherever you are
(Open arms wide.)

Eating's to everyone's liking!
(Pretend to eat.)

Book Talk

Picnic by Emily Arnold McCully. il. by author. New York: Harper & Row, 1984.
Introduce the story: "The mice family is going on a picnic. On the way one of the children falls off the truck and no one notices. At the field the rest of the family swims and plays baseball. It's only when they sit down to eat lunch that they realize the mouse child is missing. Now what will they do?"

Ernest and Celestine's Picnic by Gabrielle Vincent. il. by author. New York: Greenwillow, 1982.
Introduce the story: "Celestine is so excited about the picnic she and Ernest are planning. But then it starts to rain, to pour. Celestine wants to go on a picnic anyway. So, Ernest finds himself bundled up, walking in the rain and looking for the perfect spot for a picnic. The picnic proves to be very interesting."

The Teddy Bears' Picnic by Jimmy Kennedy. il. by Alexandra Day. La Jolla, Calif.: Green Tiger Press, 1983.

Introduce the story: "While the mice family and Celestine and Vincent had problems on their picnics, the teddy bears in this story just have fun. They play, dance, sing, and eat. But are these real bears at this picnic? Look closely."

Activities

"Picnic Item Feelies Box" developed by Paula Gaj Sitarz.

Do ahead: Get a picnic basket (a box will do) and place the following items inside: napkins, paper cup, paper plate, small bag of chips, apple, sealed pack of cookies, and wrapped sandwich. Think of other picnic items that are safe to touch and include them.

During the program: Invite each child in turn to place a hand in the box or basket and to feel the objects inside. Then ask what he or she thinks it contains. When everyone is through guessing, show the items to the children.

You might choose to end the program by giving each child a cookie or an apple to enjoy at home.

TRY THIS!

Read Aloud

Hines, Anna Grossnickle. *Come to the Meadow*. il. by author. New York: Clarion Books, 1984.

Book Talk

Denton, Kady MacDonald. *The Picnic*. il. by author. New York: E. P. Dutton, 1988.

Dubanevich, Arlene. *Pig William*. il. by author. New York: Bradbury Press, 1985.

Dunham, Meredith. *Picnic: How Do You Say It: English • French • Spanish • Italian*. il. by author. New York: Lothrop, Lee & Shepard Books, 1986.

Fisher, Aileen. *Once We Went on a Picnic*. il. by Tony Chen. New York: Thomas Y. Crowell, 1975.

Keller, Holly. *Henry's Fourth of July*. il. by author. New York: Greenwillow, 1985.

Schumacher, Claire. *Nutty's Picnic*. il. by author. New York: William Morrow, 1986.

Poetry

"The Picnic," p. 31 by Dorothy Aldis and "Ants," p. 62 by Mary Ann Hoberman in *Read-Aloud Rhymes for the Very Young* selected by Jack Prelutsky. il. by Marc Brown. New York: Alfred A. Knopf, 1986.

"Three Guests," p. 41 by Jessica Nelson North in *The Read-Aloud Treasury* compiled by Joanna Cole and Stephanie Calmenson. il. by Ann Schweninger. Garden City, N.Y.: Doubleday, 1988.

Fingerplay and Action Rhyme

"The Ant Hill" adapted as a fingerplay by Paula Gaj Sitarz from a traditional poem.

The Ant Hill

Here's the ant hill, with no ants about;
(Make fist with left hand.)

And I say, "Little ants, won't you please come out?"
(Cup hands to mouth.)

Out they come trooping in answer to my call,
One, two, three, four, five and that's all.
(Raise fingers of left hand for each number.)

"Pack the Paper Plates and Napkins," p. 168 in *Channels to Children: Early Childhood Activity Guide for Holidays and Seasons* by Carol Beckman, Roberta Simmons, and Nancy Thomas. il. by Debbie Reisbeck. Colorado Springs, Colo.: Channels to Children, 1982.

Song

"Going On a Picnic," pp. 30-31 by Georgia E. Garlid and Lynn Freeman Olson in *The Raffi Singable Songbook: A Collection of 51 Songs from Raffi's First Three Records for Young Children.* il. by Joyce Yamamoto. New York: Crown, 1987.

Wiggle and Hop:
Stories about Rabbits

PUBLICITY

Create posters and handouts in the shape of rabbit ears, a rabbit, or a carrot stick. Tack photographs of rabbits on your bulletin board or make carrots out of construction paper and staple them to your board.

PROGRAM PLAN

Do you have access to Beatrix Potter figurines or stuffed animals of Peter Rabbit, the Flopsy Bunnies, and/or Benjamin Bunny? Place them in the program area. Put stuffed toy rabbits in the area also. Set a basket of carrots by your side. Why not display a "bunny salad"? The children will be intrigued and delighted by it. Find instructions for and a photograph of "Bunny Salad" on page 57 in *Betty Crocker's New Boys and Girls Cook Book*. il. by Gloria Kamen. New York: Golden Press, 1965.

Introduction

Introduce the program: "Rabbits—white, black, brown, gray, with fluffy tails and noses that wrinkle. Have you ever seen a rabbit at a pet shop, in your yard, at the park, or in the woods? If so, they seem to live quiet, simple lives, don't they? But the rabbits we'll meet in the stories we share today lead interesting lives."

Read Aloud

Bunnies and Their Hobbies by Nancy Carlson. il. by author. Minneapolis, Minn.: Carolrhoda Books, 1984.
Introduce the story: "After bunnies spend a long day at work, after they eat dinner and wash the dishes, what do they do for fun?"

Read Aloud

Nothing Sticks Like a Shadow by Ann Tompert. il. by Lynn Munsinger. Boston: Houghton Mifflin, 1984.
Introduce the story: "Here's how another rabbit spends his free time. Woodchuck bets Rabbit his hat that Rabbit cannot get rid of his shadow. Rabbit is sure that he can lose his shadow, but can he?"

Fingerplay

"The Rabbit," p. 51 in *Listen! And Help Tell the Story* by Bernice Wells Carlson. il. by Burmah Burris. Nashville, Tenn.: Abingdon, 1965.
Introduce the fingerplay: "What would you do if you met a rabbit face to face? Would you run away or would you do what the young person in this story does?"
Demonstrate this fingerplay and then invite the children to join you. Repeat.

The Rabbit*

I saw a little rabbit come Hop, hop, hop!	(Make hopping motions with hands and arms.)
I saw his two long ears go	(Put hands at sides of head.)
Flop, flop, flop!	(Flop hands up and down.)
I saw his little nose go Twink, twink twink.	(Wiggle nose.)
I saw his little eyes go Wink, wink, wink.	(Wink eyes.)
I said, "Little Rabbit, won't you stay?"	
Then he looked at me,	(Pause and stare.)
And hopped away.	(Make fast hopping motions with hands and arms.)

Read Aloud

Henry and the Red Stripes by Eileen Christelow. il. by author. New York: Clarion Books, 1982.

Introduce the story: "Henry Rabbit paints a picture of a rabbit family with red stripes on their fur. It gives Henry the idea to paint red stripes on himself. Let's see if that's a good idea or if it gets him into trouble."

Fingerplay

"Little Bunny," p. 12 in *Ring a Ring O' Roses: Stories, Games and Finger Plays for Pre-School Children*, rev. ed. Flint, Mich.: Flint Public Library, 1981.

Introduce the fingerplay: "A short while ago we saw what happened when a young person met a rabbit. Now let's share this story on our hands about another young person who comes face to face with a rabbit."

Slowly demonstrate this for the children. Then invite them to do it with you and repeat a bit faster.

Little Bunny

There was a little bunny who
    lived in the wood.
	(Use forefingers on either
	    side of head for ears.

He wiggled his ears as a good bunny should.	Wiggle.)

He hopped by a squirrel.	(Hold up two fingers and close
	    the others on the hand and
	    hop them down other arm.)

He hopped by a tree.	(Repeat.)

---

*From *Listen! And Help Tell the Story* by Bernice Wells Carlson. Copyright © 1965 by Abingdon. Used by permission.

He hopped by a duck.	(Repeat.)
And he hopped by me.	(Hop over the opposite fist.)
He stared at the squirrel.	(Stare.)
He stared at the tree.	(Repeat.)
He stared at the duck.	
But he made faces at me!	(Wiggle nose in rabbit fashion.)

Read Aloud

The Tortoise and the Hare by Janet Stevens. il. by author. New York: Holiday House, 1984.

Introduce the story: "Rabbit is not very kind to Tortoise. He's always teasing Tortoise about how slow he is. One day Rabbit challenges Tortoise to a race. Tortoise agrees to run against Rabbit, but can he win?"

Book Talk

The Marathon Rabbit by Mike Eagle. il. by author. New York: Holt, Rinehart and Winston, 1985.

Introduce the story: "In this story you'll meet a rabbit who wants to race against people, not a tortoise. It's the day of the city marathon race. Alongside the human runners is a rabbit with a note pinned to his sweatsuit. The note says that the rabbit wants to run in the race. Should he? Can he do well against all those people?"

Book Talk

Dance Away! by George Shannon. il. by Jose Aruego and Ariane Dewey. New York: Greenwillow, 1982.

Introduce the story: "Meet a rabbit who isn't a runner but loves to dance. Everytime he sees his friends he dances with them. Rabbit's friends don't want to dance all the time, but they may change their minds after the scary thing that happens to them."

Mr. Rabbit and the Lovely Present by Charlotte Zolotow. il. by Maurice Sendak. New York: Harper & Row, 1962.

Introduce the story: "Meet a little girl who doesn't know what to get her mother for a birthday present. She asks Mr. Rabbit for help. With his advice the little girl gives her mother a beautiful present that includes something red, something orange, something yellow, something green, and something blue."

Film

Where Is It? New York: Texture Films, 1980. 3 min.

Introduce the film: "Let's join a white rabbit as it hops about looking for something delicious to eat."

Display the book: *Where Is It?* by Tana Hoban. photographs by author. New York: Macmillan, 1974.

TRY THIS!

Read Aloud

Christelow, Eileen. *Henry and the Dragon*. il. by author. Boston: Clarion Books/Ticknor & Fields: Houghton Mifflin, 1984.

Cleveland, David. *The April Rabbits*. il. by Nurit Karlin. New York: Coward, McCann & Geoghegan, 1978.

Henkes, Kevin. *Bailey Goes Camping*. il. by author. New York: Greenwillow, 1985.

Lionni, Leo. *Let's Make Rabbits: A Fable*. il. by author. New York: Pantheon, 1982.

Wahl, Jan. *Doctor Rabbit's Foundling*. il. by Cyndy Szekeres. New York: Pantheon, 1977.

Wildsmith, Brian. *The Hare and the Tortoise*. il. by author. New York: Franklin Watts, 1966.

Williams, Garth. *The Rabbit's Wedding*. il. by author. New York: Harper & Row, 1958.

Book Talk

Brown, Margaret Wise. *The Runaway Bunny*. il. by Clement Hurd. New York: Harper & Row, 1972.

Delton, Judy. *Rabbit Finds a Way*. il. by Joe Lasker. New York: Crown, 1975.

Jewell, Nancy. *The Snuggle Bunny*. il. by Mary Chalmers. New York: Harper & Row, 1972

Potter, Beatrix. *The Tale of Peter Rabbit*. il. by author. New York: Frederick Warne, 1902.

Fingerplay and Action Rhyme

"A Bunny," p. 303 in *Handbook for Storytellers* by Caroline Feller Bauer. Chicago: American Library Association, 1977.

"Bunny in the Wood," and "Ears So Funny," p. 70 in *Finger Frolics: Over 250 Fingerplays for Children from 3 Years*, rev. ed. compiled by Liz Cromwell, Dixie Hibner, and John R. Faitel. il. by Joan Lockwood. Livonia, Mich.: Partner Press, 1983.

"A Family of Rabbits," p. 5 in *Kidstuff*, vol. 1, no. 8, "Rabbits, Wabbits, Rabbits" edited by Sheila Debs. Lake Park, Fla.: GuideLines Press, 1982.

"A Little Brown Rabbit Popped Out of the Ground" adapted as a fingerplay by Paula Gaj Sitarz from a traditional poem.

"A Little Brown Rabbit Popped Out of the Ground"

A little brown rabbit popped out of the ground,
(Make fist with right hand. Open fist on word "popped.")

Wriggled his whiskers and looked around.
(Wriggle fingers.)

Another wee rabbit who lived in the grass
(Make fist with left hand.)

Popped his head out and watched him pass.
(Open left hand.)

Then both the wee rabbits went hoppity hop,
(Make fists with both hands. Hop them up and down.)

Hoppity, hoppity, hoppity hop,
(Continue to hop fists up and down.)

Till they came to a wall and had to stop.
(Stop hopping hands.)

Then both the wee rabbits turned themselves 'round,
(Twist hands at wrists.)

And scuttled off home to their holes in the ground.
(Run hands quickly behind back.)

"My Rabbit," p. 34 in *Let's Do Fingerplays* by Marion F. Grayson. il. by Nancy Weyl. Washington, D.C.: Robert B. Luce, 1962.

Film

Tortoise and the Hare. Burbank, Calif.: Disney Film Company, 1975. 8 min. 30 sec.

Rainy Days

PUBLICITY

Fashion posters and handouts in the shape of an umbrella, rain slicker, or cloud. Decorate your bulletin board with gray clouds or open umbrellas with raindrops. Maybe you would like to turn your board into a window with rain splattering the glass or transform your board into the windshield of a car with wipers.

PROGRAM PLAN

Set some umbrellas in the program area away from the children so no one gets poked accidentally. Wear a rain hat, rain slicker, and/or galoshes or place these articles of clothing near you.

Introduction

Introduce the program: "Rainy days are sometimes quiet. On rainy days you can stay cozy inside and read, color, do puzzles, or sing songs. But rainy days can also lead to amazing adventures as we'll discover in some of the stories we share today."

Poetry

"Wet" and "Mudlarks" in *Out and About* by Shirley Hughes. il. by author. New York: Lothrop, Lee & Shepard Books, 1988. unpaged.

Introduce the first poem: "What's a rainy day like? Let's hear how the writer of this poem describes a rainy day."

Introduce the second poem: "One nice thing that happens after it rains is that the dirt turns to mud. Let's hear what you can do in the mud."

Read Aloud

The Lady Who Saw the Good Side of Everything by Pat Decker Tapio. il. by Paul Galdone. New York: The Seabury Press, 1975.

Introduce the story: "The day starts out perfectly for the lady and her cat, but then it begins to rain and rain. So begins an incredible adventure which leads the lady and her cat halfway around the world."

Fingerplay

"The Rain," p. 12 by Anonymous in *Read-Aloud Rhymes for the Very Young* selected by Jack Prelutsky. il. by Marc Brown. New York: Alfred A. Knopf, 1986.

Introduce the fingerplay: "Let's pretend it's raining!"

Do the fingerplay and invite the children to join you. Do several times.

The Rain
(Adapted as a fingerplay by Paula Gaj Sitarz)

Rain on the green grass
(Hold ten fingers up straight for blades of grass.)

And rain on the tree
(Hold arms up like branches.)

And rain on the housetop
(Hands touching over head like steeple.)

But not upon me!
(Point to self.)

Song

"Rain, Rain," p. 49 in *Singing Bee! A Collection of Favorite Children's Songs*
compiled by Jane Hart. il. by Anita Lobel. New York: Lothrop, Lee &
Shepard Books, 1982.

Introduce the song: "If you ever want to chase the rain away, just sing this
song."

Sing this song for the children and then have them join you. Repeat several times.

Read Aloud

Mushroom in the Rain adapted by Mirra Ginsburg from the Russian of V.
Suteyev. il. by Jose Aruego and Ariane Dewey. New York: Macmillan,
1974.

Introduce the story: "It's raining and many animals want to stay dry under
a mushroom. Can they fit?"

Read Aloud

Henry the Castaway by Mark Taylor. il. by Graham Booth. New York: Atheneum, 1972.

Introduce the story: "Henry and his dog Laird Angus McAngus are off on
an adventure. Their trip turns scary and dangerous when a rainstorm kicks
up."

Fingerplay

"Falling Raindrops," pp. 86-87 in *Ring a Ring O' Roses: Stories, Games and
Finger Plays for Pre-School Children*, rev. ed. Flint, Mich.: Flint Public
Library, 1981.

Introduce the fingerplay: "It's raining all around us. Maybe we should use
our umbrellas so we won't get soaked."

Try this fingerplay twice with the children.

Falling Raindrops

Raindrops, raindrops! (Move fingers to imitate falling
Falling all around.   rain.
Pitter-patter on the rooftops,
Pitter-patter on the ground. (Repeat.)
Here is my umbrella.   (Pretend to open umbrella.)
It will keep me dry.   (Place over head.)
When I go walking in the rain.
I hold it up so high.   (Hold high in air.)

Book Talk

Dandelion by Don Freeman. il. by author. New York: Viking Press, 1964.
  Introduce the story: "Dandelion is so excited about Miss Giraffe's party. He gets dressed up, has his hair done, and when he knocks on Miss Giraffe's door she doesn't recognize him. Share this book with someone at home and see how a rainfall helps Dandelion get into the party."

The Rain Cloud by Mary Rayner. il. by author. New York: Atheneum, 1980.
  Introduce the story: "The rain cloud is full of rain and it must let it fall. But no one wants it to—not the children with sand castles at the beach, not people with their wash hanging out, not people at a picnic, or a man painting. The cloud doesn't want to disturb people, but isn't there anyone who wants the rain?"

Thunderstorm by Mary Szilagyi. il. by author. Scarsdale, N.Y.: Bradbury Press, 1985.
  Introduce the story: "A little girl and her dog are playing outside when the birds call to each other and thunder crackles far away. See who is most frightened by the crack, flash, boom—mother, the little girl, or the dog."

Felt-Board Story

The Hippo Boat by Eriko Kishida. il. by Chiyoko Nakatani. Cleveland, Ohio: William Collins and World Publishing, 1968.
  Introduce the story: "Let's join the animals at the zoo. A rain starts lightly. But, as it comes down more heavily this is what happens."
  You will need the following felt pieces: mother hippo, baby hippo, turtle, island, pool of water, cages, trees, rabbit family, kangaroo family, man and boat, and other zoo animals.

Activities

"Outdoors on a Rainy Day". A creative dramatics activity developed by Paula Gaj Sitarz.
  Introduce the activity: "Let's pretend that we're outside on a rainy day. What are some of the things we can do."
  Here are some suggestions for activities the entire group can act out:

- Put on a raincoat.
- Put on boots.
- Open an umbrella.
- Feel the rain as it falls on your face.
- Splash through the puddles.
- Float a boat in a puddle.
- Jump over gutters.
- Hear your feet squish in the mud. (Make squishing sounds as you walk through the mud.)
- Taste raindrops on your tongue.

TRY THIS!

Read Aloud

Burningham, John. *Mr. Gumpy's Motor Car*. il. by author. New York: Thomas Y. Crowell, 1973.

Freeman, Don. *A Rainbow of My Own*. il. by author. New York: Viking Press, 1966.

Garelick, May. *Where Does the Butterfly Go When It Rains?* il. by Leonard Weisgard. Reading, Mass.: Addision-Wesley, 1961.

Hines, Anna Grossnickle. *Taste the Raindrops*. il. by author. New York: Greenwillow, 1983.

Keats, Ezra Jack. *A Letter to Amy*. il by author. New York: Harper & Row, 1968.

Keller, Holly. *Will It Rain?* il by author. New York: Greenwillow, 1984.

Scheer, Julian. *Rain Makes Applesauce*. il. by Marvin Bileck. New York: Holiday House, 1964.

Shulevitz, Uri. *Rain Rain Rivers*. il. by author. New York: Farrar, Straus & Giroux, 1969.

Yashima, Taro. *Umbrella*. il. by author. New York: Viking Press, 1958.

Book Talk

Aardema, Verna, reteller. *Bringing the Rain to Kapiti Plain*. il. by Beatriz Vidal. New York: Dial Books for Young Readers, 1981.

Blegvad, Lenore. *Rainy Day Kate*. il. by Erik Blegvad. New York: Margaret K. McElderry Books/Macmillan, 1987.

Ferro, Beatriz. *Caught in the Rain*. il. by Michele Sambin. Garden City, N.Y.: Doubleday, 1980.

Iwasaki, Chihiro. *Staying Home Alone on a Rainy Day.* il. by author. New York: McGraw-Hill, 1968.

Kalan, Robert. *Rain.* il. by Donald Crews. New York: Greenwillow, 1978.

Murphy, Shirley Rousseau. *Tattie's River Journey.* il. by Tomie dePaola. New York: Dial Press, 1983.

Ryder, Joanne. *A Wet and Sandy Day.* il. by Donald Carrick. New York: Harper & Row, 1977.

Skofield, James. *All Wet! All Wet!* il. by Diane Stanley. New York: Harper & Row, 1984.

Spier, Peter. *Peter Spier's Rain.* il. by author. Garden City, N.Y.: Doubleday, 1982. (This is a wordless book.)

Other Story Forms

"Rain on the Green Grass," p. 306 in *Handbook for Storytellers* by Caroline Feller Bauer. Chicago: American Library Association, 1977. (This is a fold-and-cut story.)

"A Rainy Day." pp. 22-23 in *Tell and Draw Stories* by Margaret J. Olson. Minneapolis, Minn.: Creative Storytime Press, 1963.

Poetry

"Galoshes," p. 18 by Rhoda Bacmeister in *Sing a Song of Popcorn: Every Child's Book of Poems* selected by Beatrice Schenk de Regniers, Eva Moore, Mary Michaels White, and Jan Carr. il. by nine Caldecott Medal artists. New York: Scholastic, 1988.
(Have the children pretend to walk in the puddles and mud as you read this poem.)

"Rain," by Robert Louis Stevenson and from "The Umbrella Brigade" by Laura E. Richards, p. 46 in *The Read-Aloud Treasury* compiled by Joanna Cole and Stephanie Calmenson. il. by Ann Schweninger. Garden City, N.Y.: Doubleday, 1988.

"Rainy Rainy Saturday," pp. 6-7 in *Rainy Rainy Saturday* by Jack Prelutsky. il. by Marilyn Hafner. New York: Greenwillow, 1980.

"Showers," p. 12 and "Rainy Day," p. 13 in *Read-Aloud Rhymes for the Very Young* selected by Jack Prelutsky. il. Marc Brown. New York: Alfred A. Knopf, 1986.

"Spring Rain," p. 42 by Marchette Chute in *The Random House Book of Poetry for Children: A Treasury of 572 Poems for Today's Child* selected by Jack Prelutsky. il. by Arnold Lobel. New York: Random House, 1983.

Fingerplay and Action Rhyme

"Boom, Bang!" and "Puddle Magic" in *Little Boy Blue: Finger Plays Old and New* by Daphne Hogstrom. il. by Alice Schlesinger. Racine, Wis.: Western Publishing, 1966. unpaged.

Little Raindrops," p. 88 and "Puddle Magic" and "Rainy Day Fun," p. 89 in *Ring a Ring O' Roses: Stories, Games and Finger Plays for Pre-School Children*, rev. ed. Flint, Mich.: Flint Public Library, 1981.

"Pitter Patter Goes the Rain," p. 49 in *Listen! And Help Tell the Story* by Bernice Wells Carlson. il. by Burmah Burris. Nashville, Tenn.: Abingdon, 1965.

"Pitter-Patter Raindrops," p. 21 in *Stamp Your Feet: Action Rhymes* chosen by Sarah Hayes. il. by Toni Goffe. New York: Lothrop, Lee & Shepard Books, 1988.

Song

"Ducks Like Rain," pp. 62-63 in *The 2nd Raffi Songbook*. piano arrangements by Catherine Ambrose. design and illustrations by Joyce Yamamoto. New York: Crown, 1986.

"If All the Raindrops," pp. 140-141 in *The Fireside Book of Children's Songs* collected and edited by Marie Winn. musical arrangements by Allan Miller. il. by John Alcorn. New York: Simon & Schuster, 1966.

School Days

PUBLICITY

Grab everyone's attention with handouts and posters cut in the shape of a ruler, pencil, crayon, or apple. Tack the letters "A,B,C," the numbers "1,2,3," and various shapes to your bulletin board.

PROGRAM PLAN

If your program takes place in a nonschool setting, suggest a school atmosphere with the following items: a blackboard and a small table with paper, crayons, pencil, eraser, paint and brush, and a pad of paper.

Take the stories you share with the children out of a book bag. Place a lap desk near you with an apple on it.

Introduction

Invite the children to share stories with you about their experiences in nursery school or kindergarten. Then continue: "We'll meet many school children in the stories we share today. Let's see what their school days are like."

Read Aloud

My Teacher Sleeps in School by Leatie Weiss. il. by Ellen Weiss. New York: Frederick Warne, 1984.

Introduce the story: "Mollie has decided that her teacher lives at school —eats, bathes, and sleeps there. The teacher must live in school because she's always there before the children come in the morning and she stays after they go home for the day. Doesn't that make sense? But where would the teacher eat and sleep in the school? Can Mollie and her classmates figure it out?"

Song

"Good Morning to You," p. 115 by Mildred J. Hill in *Singing Bee! A Collection of Favorite Children's Songs* compiled by Jane Hart. il. by Anita Lobel. New York: Lothrop, Lee & Shepard Books, 1982.

Introduce the song: "Some children sing this song to their teachers at school in the morning. Let's share the song now."

This song has the same melody as "Happy Birthday" so the children will be familiar with it. Try it several times with the group.

Read Aloud

Miss Nelson Is Missing by Harry Allard. il. by James Marshall. Boston: Houghton Mifflin, 1977.

Introduce the story: "The children in Miss Nelson's class are being terrible. They're throwing paper airplanes, making faces, and not listening to Miss Nelson. What can she do about the children's awful behavior?"

Action Rhyme

"School Days" by Paula Gaj Sitarz.

Introduce the rhyme. "What do you do during the day at school? Here's a rhyme about some children who go to nursery school. They have a lot of fun. Let's join them now."

This rhyme, which has many broad motions, can be done seated. Demonstrate first and then invite the children to join you. Repeat.

School Days

Teacher holds the door open.
(Swing arm out wide.)

Everyone says hello.
(Wave.)

We hang our coats on hooks.
(Imitate hanging coat.)

Now there's fun you know.

I play trucks with Jennifer.
(Imitate moving truck with hand.)

Then we eat our snack.
(Pretend to eat.)

Teacher reads a story.
(Hands held open to represent book.)

Then we sing and clap.
(Clap hands.)

Some days we paint.
(Pretend to paint.)

Sometimes we cook dough.
(Put dough in oven.)

Then we clean up.
(Dusting motion with hand.)

And get ready to go.
(Pretend to put on coat.)

Read Aloud

Will I Have a Friend? by Miriam Cohen. il. by Lillian Hoban. New York: Macmillan, 1967.

Introduce the story: "Jim is a little nervous when he goes to school for the first time. He asks his dad if he will have a friend. Dad says he will, but who will be Jim's friend? Will it be Anna-Maria, Joseph, or maybe George?"

Read Aloud

The Day the Teacher Went Bananas by James Howe. il. by Lillian Hoban.
New York: E. P. Dutton, 1984.
Introduce the story: "Meet the children in this classroom who have a new teacher. He's unlike any teacher I've seen. He grunts and eats sixteen bananas for lunch. What can he teach the children?"

Activities

"Simon Says"
Introduce the activity: "Children learn a lot in school but there's also time for recess and play. So let's play a game now."
Be sure the children have room to move about. Explain that they are only to do the actions that "Simon Says." If they hear a command without "Simon Says," they shouldn't do it. Keep this noncompetitive. Don't make children "drop out" of the game if they move when they aren't supposed to. Simply go on and play as long as the children are interested.
Here are some suggested actions:

- Simon says clap your hands.
- Simon says hop on one foot.
- Jump up and down.
- Simon says flap your arms.
- Laugh.
- Simon says roar like a lion.
- Simon says touch your toes.
- Simon says take one step forward.
- Quack like a duck.
- Wriggle your nose.
- Simon says turn around.
- Simon says raise your left hand.
- Sing a song.
- Simon says sit down.

Hand out a bookmark or an apple to each child at the end of the program.

TRY THIS!

Read Aloud

Bucknall, Caroline. *One Bear in the Picture*. il. by author. New York: Dial Books for Young Readers, 1987.

Cazet, Denys. *A Fish in His Pocket*. il by author. New York: Orchard Books, 1987.

Charmatz, Bill. *The Troy St. Bus*. il. by author. New York: Macmillan, 1977.

Isadora, Rachel. *Willaby*. il. by author. New York: Macmillan, 1977.

Mahy, Margaret. *The Boy Who Was Followed Home*. il. by Steven Kellogg, New York: Franklin Watts, 1975.

Book Talk

Feder, Paula Kurzband. *Where Does the Teacher Live?* il. by Lillian Hoban. New York: E. P. Dutton, 1979.

Goodall, John. *Naughty Nancy Goes to School*. il. by author. New York: Margaret K. McElderry/Atheneum, 1985.

Lindgren, Astrid. *I Want to Go to School Too*. il. by Ilon Wikland. translated from Swedish by Barbara Lucas. New York: R & S Books, 1987.

McCully, Emily Arnold. *School*. il. by author. New York: Harper & Row, 1987. (This is a wordless book.)

Wells, Rosemary. *Timothy Goes to School*. il. by author. New York: Dial Press, 1981.

Yashima, Taro. *Crow Boy*. il. by author. New York: Viking Press, 1955.

Fingerplay and Action Rhyme

"My Teacher," p. 80 in *Finger Frolics: Over 250 Fingerplays for Children from 3 Years*, rev. ed. compiled by Liz Cromwell, Dixie Hibner, and John R. Faitel. il. by Joan Lockwood. Livonia, Mich.: Partner Press, 1983.

Film

Miss Nelson Is Missing. New York: Learning Corporation of America, 1979. 14 min.

Sea and Seashore

PUBLICITY

Decorate your posters and handouts with items associated with the beach. If you prefer, cut out posters and handouts in the shape of a beach pail, beach towel, seashell, or swimsuit. Create a sea scene on your bulletin board or decorate it with seashells cut out of construction paper.

PROGRAM PLAN

Turn your story area into a beach. Invite the children to sit on blankets or beach towels. Surround them with pails, shovels, sifters, and a cooler. Do you have a toy boat, float, or inner tube to add? Maybe you have a fish net or some seashells. You might like to sit on a beach towel or wear a pair of flippers or thongs. If you think all of these items would distract the children, select only a few for the program space.

Introduction

Your opening comments will depend on whether or not the children in your program live near a beach or have ever been to a beach.

Book Talk

Briefly talk about the next three books.

Down to the Beach by May Garelick. il. by Barbara Cooney. New York: Four Winds Press, 1973.
Show the illustrations in this book which depict children building sand castles, swimming, looking for shells and hermit crabs, and burying someone in the sand.

Beach Days by Ken Robbins. photographs by author. New York: Viking Kestrel, 1987.
Share the photographs of people riding the waves, trying to catch the wind, and building sand castles.

Let's Discover the Seaside by Maria Rius. il. by J. M. Parramon. Woodbury, N.Y.: Barron's Educational Series, 1986.
The children will enjoy seeing the illustrations of fishermen with their nets, ocean liners, and sea gulls soaring.

Read Aloud

Come Again, Pelican by Don Freeman. il. by author. New York: Viking Press, 1961.
Introduce the story: "Every year Ty and his family camp in the dunes by the ocean. And every year Ty's friend, a pelican, is there to greet him. This year Ty tells the pelican that he's going to catch some fish. But that isn't all Ty ends up doing."

Fingerplay

"Ocean Shell," p. 6 in *Ring a Ring O' Roses: Stories, Games and Finger Plays for Children*, rev. ed. Flint, Mich.: Flint Public Library, 1981.

Introduce the fingerplay: "Ty had quite an adventure when he went fishing at the beach. Maybe he should have collected seashells instead. It's fun to do and very safe. Let's collect some now."

Show the children how to do this fingerplay and then have them join you. Repeat.

Ocean Shell

I found a great big shell one day.
Upon the ocean floor.

(Hold hands cupped as if holding large shell.)

I held it close up to my ear.
I heard the ocean roar!

(Raise hands to ear.)

I found a tiny little shell one day.
Upon the ocean sand

(One hand cupped as if holding little shell.)

The waves had worn it nice and smooth.

(Pretend to roll shell between palms of both hands.)

It felt nice in my hand.

Read Aloud

Harry By the Sea by Gene Zion. il. by Margaret Bloy Graham. New York: Harper & Row, 1965.

Introduce the story: "Harry is at the beach with the family but he does not like the hot sun. He's sitting by the water's edge, tired from trying to find some shade, when a big wave crashes on top of him. Once the wave rolls back, Harry's quiet, relaxing day at the beach ends and his troubles begin."

Fingerplay

"Five Little Fishes," p. 5 in *Ring a Ring O' Roses: Stories, Games and Finger Plays for Children*, rev. ed. Flint, Mich.: Flint Public Library, 1981.

Introduce the fingerplay: "While people like Ty and animals like Harry are busy at the shoreline, fish are scurrying about in the water. Let's join them now."

This is an easy counting rhyme so the children can try it with you without a demonstration.

Five Little Fishes

Five little fishes were swimming near the shore.
One took a dive, then there were four.

(Hold up five fingers. Starting with thumb, bend down one at a time as verse progresses.)

Four little fishes were
    swimming out to sea.
One went for food, then there
    were three.
Three little fishes said:
"Now what shall we do?"
One swam away, and then there
    were two.
Two little fishes were having
    great fun.
But one took a plunge,
Then there was one.
One little fish said:
"I like the warm sun."
Away he went and then there
    were none."   (Put hand behind back.)

Read Aloud

Mice at the Beach by Haruo Yamashita. il. by Kazuo Iwamura. New York:
    William Morrow, 1987.
    Introduce the story: "Let's join Mama Mouse, Papa Mouse, and the seven
mice children as they enjoy a day at the beach. Papa Mouse should watch out.
He's so busy keeping track of his children that he doesn't pay attention to
what's happening to him."

Read Aloud

Sand Cake by Frank Asch. il. by author. New York: Parents Magazine Press,
    1979.
    Introduce the story: "Baby Bear is worried. He agreed to eat the cake his
father plans to make on the beach. How can his father bake a cake with
nothing but sand all around? And how will Baby Bear eat this cake?"

Song

"There's a Hole in the Bottom of the Sea," p. 78-79 in *Eye Winker, Tom
    Tinker, Chin Chopper* by Tom Glazer. il. by Ron Himler. Garden City,
    N.Y.: Doubleday, 1973.
    Introduce the song: "You never know what you might find at the bottom
of the sea. Let's jump in and take a journey underwater to see something
unusual."
    Try this on the felt board while you sing it. You will need the following
items made of felt: a hole, a log, a bump, a frog, a wart, a hair, a flea, and a
germ.

Activities

"A Day at the Beach." A creative dramatics activity developed by Paula Gaj
    Sitarz.

Introduce the activity: "We shared many stories about the seashore today. Now let's pretend that we're at the beach having fun."

Mention each activity and let the children interpret it. Then suggest your own interpretation.

Try these activities:

- Fly a kite.
- Bury someone in the sand.
- Soar like a sea gull.
- Collect shells.
- Feed the birds.
- Swim and splash.
- Fish.
- Catch a crab.
- Spread a towel on the sand.
- Jump in the waves.
- Make a sand castle.
- Run along the shore.
- Sit on a rock.
- Fill your pockets with shells.
- Rub suntan lotion on yourself.
- Eat a snack.
- Put on sunglasses.
- Row a boat.
- Open an umbrella.
- Dig a hole in the sand.
- Rake seaweed.
- Turn on a radio.

TRY THIS!

Read Aloud

Brown, Marc. *D. W. All Wet*. il. by author. Boston: Joy Street Books/Little, Brown, 1988.

Cohen, Caron Lee. *Whiffle Squeek*. il. by Ted Rand. New York: Dodd, Mead, 1987.

Hutchins, Pat. *One-Eyed Jake*. il. by author. New York: Greenwillow, 1979.

Lindgren, Barbro. *The Wild Baby Goes to Sea*. il. by Eva Erikson. adapted from the Swedish by Jack Prelutsky. New York: Greenwillow, 1983.

Lionni, Leo. *Swimmy*. il. by author. New York: Pantheon, 1963.

Rockwell, Anne F., and Harlow Rockwell. *At the Beach*. il. by authors. New York: Macmillan, 1987.

Book Talk

Burningham, John. *Come Away from the Water, Shirley*. il. by author. New York: Thomas Y. Crowell, 1977.

Gebert, Warren. *The Old Ball and the Sea*. il. by author. Scarsdale, N.Y.: Bradbury Press, 1988.

Goodall, John S. *Paddy under Water*. il. by author. New York: Atheneum, 1985. (This is a wordless book.)

Jonas, Ann. *Reflections*. il. by author. New York: Greenwillow, 1987.

Ryder, Joanne. *A Wet and Sandy Day*. il. by Donald Carrick. New York: Harper & Row, 1977.

Turkle, Brinton. *The Sky Dog*. il. by author. New York: Viking Press, 1969.

Other Story Forms

"The Big Fish," pp. 9-19 in *Tell and Draw Stories* by Margaret J. Olson. Minneapolis, Minn.: Creative Storytime Press, 1963.

"The Fish with the Deep Sea Smile," pp. 146-151 a poem by Margaret Wise Brown in *The Flannel Board Storytelling Book* by Judy Sierra. Chicago: H. W. Wilson, 1987.

Poetry

"The Sailor Song," p. 65 in *The Read-Aloud Treasury* by Joanna Cole and Stephanie Calmenson. il. by Ann Schweninger. Garden City, N.Y.: Doubleday, 1988.

"Sand" and "Seaside" in *Out and About* by Shirley Hughes. il. by author. New York: Lothrop, Lee & Shepard Books, 1988. unpaged.

"Shore," p. 30 by Mary Britton Miller and "Fish," p. 44 by Mary Ann Hoberman in *Read-Aloud Rhymes for the Very Young* selected by Jack Prelutsky. il. by Marc Brown. New York: Alfred A. Knopf, 1986.

Fingerplay and Action Rhyme

"Day at the Beach," p. 86 in *Ring a Ring O' Roses: Stories, Games and Finger Plays for Pre-School Children*, rev. ed. Flint, Mich.: Flint Public Library, 1981.

"Fishes," p. 37 in *Finger Plays and Action Rhymes* by Frances E. Jacobs. photographs by Lura and Courtney Owen. New York: Lothrop, Lee & Shepard Books, 1941.

"Five Little Children," p. 4 and "We're Going to the Beach," p. 5 in *Kidstuff*, vol. 3, no. 3, "We Are Going to the Beach", edited by Sheila Debs. Lake Park, Fla.: GuideLines Press, 1984.

"The Little Fish," p. 28 in *Listen! And Help Tell the Story* by Bernice Wells Carlson. il. by Burmah Burris. Nashville, Tenn.: Abingdon, 1965.

"The Ringdinkydoo," and "Sand Castles" in *My Big Book of Finger Plays: A Fun-to-Say, Fun-to-Play Collection* by Daphne Hogstrom. il. by Sally Augustiny. Racine, Wis.: Western Publishing, 1974. unpaged.

"Row, Row, Row," in *Little Boy Blue: Finger Plays Old and New* by Daphne Hogstrom. il. by Alice Schlesinger. Racine, Wis.: Western Publishing, 1966. unpaged.

"Ten Little Fishes," p. 96 in *With a Deep Sea Smile* by Virginia A. Tashjian. il. by Rosemary Wells. Boston: Little, Brown, 1974.

Songs

"At the Beach," p. 5 in *Kidstuff*, vol. 3, no. 3, "We Are Going to the Beach," edited by Sheila Debs. Lake Park, Fla.: GuideLines Press, 1984.

"Charlie Over the Water," p. 18 in *Eye Winker, Tom Tinker, Chin Chopper* by Tom Glazer. il. by Ron Himler. Garden City, N.Y.: Doubleday, 1973.

"Merrily We Roll Along," p. 59 and "Three White Gulls," p. 97 in *Singing Bee! A Collection of Favorite Children's Songs* compiled by Jane Hart. il. by Anita Lobel. New York: Lothrop, Lee & Shepard Books, 1982.

"Octopus's Garden," pp. 75-76 by Richard Starkey in *The 2nd Raffi Songbook*. piano arrangements by Catherine Ambrose. design and illustration by Joyce Yamamoto. New York: Crown, 1986.

Films

Neptune's Nonsense. Burbank, Calif.: Walt Disney Company, 1938. 8 min.

Swimmy. New York: Italtoons Corporation, 1968. 6 min.

I Like You:
Valentine's Day Stories

You can combine this material with the program on friends or use it as is. Children this age usually don't like "mushy" stories. But, there are some good Valentine's Day stories that concentrate on friendship between a child and a pet or a child and a relative that are enjoyable to share with preschoolers.

PUBLICITY

Draw smiling faces on your handouts and posters or decorate them with hearts or the many commercial stickers that are available for Valentine's Day. If you like, cut out posters and handouts in the shape of Hershey's Kisses. Turn your bulletin board into a giant Valentine's Day card or decorate it with hearts.

PROGRAM PLAN

Hang paper hearts or giant paper Hershey Kisses from the ceiling.

Introduction

Introduce the program: "Do you know what Valentine's Day is? It's a day to let your favorite people know how much you like them. You might give your mom a special hug on that day or give your friend a special handshake or a Valentine's Day card. You might even like to give your pet an extra treat."

Read Aloud

Freckles and Willie by Margery Cuyler. il. by Marsha Winborn. New York: Holt, Rinehart and Winston, 1986.
Introduce the story: "Freckles the dog is Willie's best friend. Freckles is always there when Willie is cold or sad. Valentine's Day is coming and Willie wants to let Freckles know how much he loves him. But a new girl moves into the neighborhood and Willie begins to forget about Freckles."

Read Aloud

One Zillion Valentines by Frank Modell. il. by author. New York: Greenwillow, 1981.
Introduce the story: "Marvin likes Valentine's Day very much so he decides to make Valentine's Day cards with his friend Milton. But they make so many cards. What will they do with them?"

Fingerplay

"Valentine's Day," p. 61 in *Ring a Ring O' Roses: Stories, Games and Finger Plays for Children*, rev. ed. Flint, Mich.: Flint Public Library, 1981.
Introduce the fingerplay: "Valentine's Day cards come in all shapes and sizes. Let's meet some now."
This is an easy counting rhyme so invite the children to join you immediately. Repeat.

Valentine's Day

Five little valentines were
    having a race.
The first little valentine
    was frilly with lace.
The second little valentine had
    a funny face.
The third little valentine
    said, "I love you."
The fourth little valentine
    said, "I do, too."
The fifth little valentine
    was sly as a fox.
He ran the fastest to your
    valentine box.

(Holding up five fingers, suit
    actions to words.)

Read Aloud

Danny's Mystery Valentine by Edith Kunhardt. il. by author. New York:
    Greenwillow, 1987.
    Introduce the story: "Danny the alligator finds a valentine on his bedroom
floor. It's not signed so Danny doesn't know who sent it to him. He's
determined to find out, though."

Poetry

Selections from *It's Valentine's Day* by Jack Prelutsky. il. by Yossi Abolafia.
    New York: Greenwillow, 1983.

"I Made My Dog a Valentine," pp. 17-19.
    Introduce the poem: "Have you ever made a valentine for a pet? The boy
in this poem did, several times, and this is what happened."

"My Special Cake," pp. 23-27.
    Introduce the poem: "The young boy in this poem decides to make a
special cake for Valentine's Day, but something goes wrong."
    Do this poem on the felt board, putting all the ingredients in a bowl. You
will need felt pieces including: bowl, butter, licorice, jelly beans, eggs, rice,
chocolate chips, peanut brittle, salt, sugar, flour, milk, raisins, and the gooey
results in a bowl.

"My Father's Valentine," pp. 42-45.
    Introduce the poem: "The young boy in this poem is making a valentine
for his dad. It's not easy to do."
    Type the poem and place it on your lap so your hands are free to cut and
recut a valentine made out of construction paper like the boy in the poem.

Read Aloud

The Mysterious Valentine by Nancy Carlson. il. by author. Minneapolis,
    Minn.: Carolrhoda, 1985.

Introduce the story: "Louanne Pig has the same problem as Danny the alligator: She's received a valentine and she doesn't know who it's from. Louanne has a clue, though. The card was signed with green ink. Who has a green pen? Someone at school, maybe?"

Book Talk

Arthur's Valentine by Marc Brown. il. by author. Boston: Little, Brown, 1980.
Introduce the story: "Valentine's Day is here and Arthur is receiving notes from someone who likes him. Who can it be? Do you think Arthur will guess who is sending these messages?"

"*Bee My Valentine*" by Miriam Cohen. il. by Lillian Hoban. New York: Greenwillow, 1978.
Introduce the story: "The children in this first-grade class are getting ready for the St. Valentine's Day party. One of the things they'll do is send each other special cards to say, 'I like you.' It sounds easy, but sending cards causes problems."

Valentine Friends by Ann Schweninger. il. by author. New York: Viking Kestrel, 1988.
Introduce the story: "Join two rabbit friends as they get ready to give a Valentine's Day party for their families. It's fun, from making invitations to baking goodies. Join the guests at the puppet show and follow everyone on the trail of hearts."

Activities

"A Valentine Relay Race," pp. 33-37 in *Things to Make and Do for Valentine's Day* by Tomie dePaola. il. by author. New York: Franklin Watts, 1976.
Introduce the book: "If you have a Valentine's Day party use this book. It's full of ideas for food to eat, games to play, and ways to get ready for your party."
To play the relay race you need a large space. Divide the players into two teams. On paper hearts write words that tell the children to move in a certain way. Include words like "hop," "crawl," and "walk backward." Put the hearts in two piles in front of the two teams. Each player picks a heart and moves in the manner suggested. Play until both teams finish. Keep it noncompetitive and fun.
Hand out Valentine's Day cards to the children when they leave. You might like to recite this rhyme as you do:

"Valentines," p. 61 in *Ring a Ring O' Roses: Stories, Games and Finger Plays for Pre-School Children*, rev. ed. Flint, Mich.: Flint Public Library, 1981.

Valentines

Valentines, valentines. Red, white and blue.
I'll find a nice one and give it to you.

TRY THIS!

Read Aloud

Devlin, Wende, and Harry Devlin. *Cranberry Valentine*. il. by authors. New York: Four Winds Press, 1986.

Book Talk

Adams, Adrienne. *The Great Valentine's Day Balloon Race*. il. by author. New York: Scribner's, 1980.

Bond, Felicia. *Four Valentines in a Rainstorm*. il. by author. New York: Thomas Y. Crowell, 1983.

Bunting, Eve. *The Valentine Bears*. il. by Jan Brett. New York: Clarion Books, 1983.

Other Story Forms

"Roses Are Red," p. 308 in *Handbook for Storytellers* by Caroline Feller Bauer. Chicago.: American Library Association, 1977. (This is a fold-and-cut story.)

Fingerplay and Action Rhyme

"Five Pretty Valentines," p. 53 in *Fingerpuppets, Fingerplays and Holidays* by Betty Keefe. Omaha, Nebr.: Special Literature Press, 1984.

"Gay Valentines" and "A Mailbox Valentine," p. 69 in *Finger Frolics: Over 250 Fingerplays for Children from 3 Years*, rev. ed. compiled by Liz Cromwell, Dixie Hibner, and John R. Faitel. il. by Joan Lockwood. Livonia, Mich.: Partner Press, 1983.

"I'll Cut Red Paper into A Heart," "A Piece of Bright Red Paper," "To Each and Every Friend of Mine," and "I Feel Topsy," p. 95 in *Channels to Children: Early Childhood Activity for Holidays and Seasons* by Carol Beckman, Roberta Simmons, and Nancy Thomas. il. by Debbie Reisbeck. Colorado Springs, Colo.: Channels to Children, 1982.

Songs

"A-Tisket, A-Tasket," pp. 12-13 in *If You're Happy and You Know It: Eighteen Story Songs* set to pictures by Nicki Weiss. music arranged by John Krumich. New York: Greenwillow, 1987.

Activities

"A-Tisket, A-Tasket," p. 12 in *Party Rhymes* collected by Marc Brown. il. by author. New York: E. P. Dutton, 1988.

"Pass the Queen's Red-Hot Heart Game," p. 37 in *The Little Witch's Valentine Book* by Linda Glovach. il. by author. Englewood Cliffs, N.J.: Prentice-Hall, 1984.

Let's Go to the Zoo

PUBLICITY

Draw the gates of a zoo on your handouts and posters or decorate them with animals found in a zoo. A collage of zoo animals found on a bulletin board is a colorful invitation to your program. Find excellent color photographs of zoo animals in back issues of *Your Big Backyard, Ranger Rick*, and *National Geographic World*, all excellent nature magazines for children. You might display your own photographs from a visit to the zoo.

PROGRAM PLAN

Do you have any toy stuffed lions, monkeys, elephants, or other animals found in a zoo to display in the story area?

Introduction

Invite the children to discuss any trips they've made to a zoo.

Book Talk

Zoo by Gail Gibbons. il. by author. New York: Thomas Y. Crowell, 1987.
Share the illustrations in this book which show the people who feed the animals, how food is prepared in the zoo's kitchen, how the cages are cleaned, where zoo babies are born, and how sick animals are cared for.

Read Aloud

Bruno Munari's Zoo by Bruno Munari. il. by author. New York: World Publishing Company, 1963.
Introduce the story: "Let's take a trip to a zoo. Follow the signs and you will see camels, zebras, monkeys, tigers, and much more."

Read Aloud

Be Nice to Spiders by Margaret Bloy Graham. il. by author. New York: Harper & Row, 1967.
Introduce the story: "When Helen the Spider is left at the zoo, the zoo keeper doesn't realize how important she is. How can a wee spider make the zoo animals happy?"

Song

"Going to the Zoo," pp. 32-33 by Tom Paxton in *The Raffi Singable Songbook: A Collection of 51 Songs from Raffi's First Three Records for Young Children*. il. by Joyce Yamamoto. New York: Crown, 1987.
Introduce the song: "We've been talking about zoos. Now let's sing a song about going to the zoo. What will we see there?"
Teach the children the easy refrain in this song.

Read Aloud

Zoo Song by Barbara Bottner. il. by Lynn Munsinger. New York: Scholastic, 1987.

Introduce the story: "Fabio, Herman, and Gertrude are neighbors at the zoo. This is the story of what happens the day Herman the lion can't stand the way Gertrude the hippo sings for one more minute, and Fabio the bear can't stand Herman being upset."

Read Aloud

Sam Who Never Forgets by Eve Rice. il. by author. New York: Greenwillow, 1977.

Introduce the story: "Let's visit another zoo. Sam is the zoo keeper there and every day at three o'clock he feeds the animals. But today is different. Did Sam forget to feed someone?"

Participation Book

A Children's Zoo by Tana Hoban. photographs by author. New York: Greenwillow, 1985.

Introduce the book: "Let's visit another zoo. There are clues in this book, so you can guess which animals live there."

Read the descriptive words which describe each animal. Give the children time to guess what animal the writer is talking about and then show the picture of the animal on the next page.

Felt-Board Story

The Hippo Boat by Eriko Kishida. il. by Chiyoko Nakatani. Cleveland, Ohio: William Collins and World Publishing, 1968.

Introduce the story: "What is happening at this zoo? It's starting to rain, harder and harder. What will the animals do? Can Mother Hippo and Baby Hippo help?"

See the list of felt pieces required in the program plan for "Rainy Days."

Film

The Mole in the Zoo. New York: Phoenix Films & Video, 1974. 10 min.

Introduce the film: "Watch Mole as he goes from one crazy adventure to another at the zoo. Wait until he lands in the lion's cage. What will happen to Mole then?"

TRY THIS!

Read Aloud

Brandenberg, Franz. *Leo and Emily's Zoo*. il. by Yossi Abolafia. New York: Greenwillow, 1988.

Cutler, Ivor. *The Animal House*. il. by Helen Oxenbury. New York: William Morrow, 1977.

De Regniers, Beatrice Schenk. *May I Bring a Friend?* il. by Beni Montresor. New York: Atheneum, 1964.

Book Talk

Fatio, Louise. *Happy Lion*. il. by author. New York: McGraw-Hill, 1954.

Kishida, Eriko. *Hippopotamus*. il. by Chiyoko Nakatani. translated from the Japanese by Masako Matsuno. Englewood Cliffs, N.J.: Prentice-Hall 1963.

Other Story Forms

"Albert's Vacation," pp. 11-14 in *More Tell and Draw Stories* by Margaret J. Olson. Minneapolis, Minn.: Arts & Crafts Unlimited, 1969.

"Jimmy and Johnny," pp. 17-19 and "Eke and Zeke," pp. 30-32 in *Tell and Draw Stories* by Margaret J. Olson. Minneapolis, Minn.: Creative Story-time Press, 1963.

Poetry

"At the Zoo," p. 35 by A. A. Milne in *Poems to Read to the Very Young* selected by Josette Frank. il. by Eloise Wilkin. New York: Random House, 1982.

"Before the Monkey's Cage," by Edna Becker and "When You Talk to a Monkey," p. 22 by Rowena Bennett, and "Giraffe's Don't Huff," p. 58 by Karla Kuskin in *Read-Aloud Rhymes for the Very Young* selected by Jack Prelutsky. il. by Marc Brown. New York: Alfred A. Knopf, 1986.

"Monkey Haven," p. 93 by Gertrude Keyworth in *Pocket Full of Posies* compiled and written by Gertrude Keyworth. il. by Jerry Ryle and Lorraine Conaway. cover designed and drawn by Joni Adam. Flint, Mich.: Flint Public Library, 1984.

Fingerplay and Action Rhyme

"Five Little Monkeys," p. 4 in *Kidstuff*, vol. 4, no. 2, "Monkeyshines" edited by Sheila Debs. Lake Park, Fla.: GuideLines Press, 1986.

"Seals," p. 77 and "Five Little Polar Bears," and "The Yellow Giraffe," p. 78 in *Finger Frolics: Over 250 Fingerplays for Children from 3 Years*, rev. ed. compiled by Liz Cromwell, Dixie Hibner, and John R. Faitel. il. by Joan Lockwood. Livonia, Mich.: Partner Press, 1983.

"Two Little Zebras," and "Two Peacocks," p. 4 in *Kidstuff*, vol. 4, no. 12, "At the Zoo" edited by Sheila Debs. Lake Park, Fla.: GuideLines Press, 1987.

Song

"The Zoo," pp. 78-81 in *Music for Ones and Twos: Songs and Games for the Very Young Child* by Tom Glazer. il. by Karen Ann Weinhaus. Garden City, N.Y.: Doubleday, 1983.

Film

Balthazar the Lion. Ossining, N.Y.: WOMBAT Productions, 1973. 12 min.

A Zoo's Eye View: Dawn to Dusk. Chicago: Encyclopedia Britannica Educational Corp., 1973. 11 min.

Activities

"Monkey See, Monkey Do," p. 5 in *Kidstuff*, vol. 1, no. 2, "Razzle Dazzle Circus," edited by Sheila Debs. Lake Park, Fla.: GuideLines Press, 1981.

Resources and Aids

The following is a selective list of books and periodicals that have proved useful in planning and executing picture book story hours.

Bauer, Caroline. *Handbook for Storytellers*. Chicago: American Library Association, 1977.

Bauer's handbook is full of ideas for planning, publicizing, and executing programs for children of all ages, especially elementary level. Part Three is particularly useful in planning story hours for preschoolers. You'll find fairly comprehensive instructions on making and presenting board stories—chalk, felt, and magnetic. If you plan to make and use puppets or to do creative dramatics and fold-and-cut stories in your programs, refer to this book. There are also bibliographies throughout the text that direct you to other detailed books written on a particular type of activity.

Brown, Marc. *Finger Rhymes*. il. by author. New York: E. P. Dutton, 1980.

Brown, Marc. *Hand Rhymes*. il. by author. New York: E. P. Dutton, 1985.

These two small collections of fingerplays contain old favorites and some less familiar rhymes. Subjects include animals, holidays, and the seasons. Each rhyme has instructions for use as a fingerplay in the form of easy-to-follow diagrams. What distinguishes these collections are the double-page illustrations that complement each rhyme. They are whimsical, detailed black-and-white drawings that are perfect to show to a group of children when you read each rhyme aloud.

Brown, Marc. *Party Rhymes*. il. by author. New York: E. P. Dutton, 1988.

Most of the rhymes in this small collection are circle games that are best used at the end of your programs. Many of them include their song versions which can be enjoyed at any point in your program. Use these rhymes in such programs as "parties," "Valentine's Day," and "houses."

Brown, Marc. *Play Rhymes*. il. by author. New York: E. P. Dutton, 1987.

This collection of fingerplays and action rhymes includes lively, playful, and humorous color illustrations. Music is included for several selections. Use these rhymes in a variety of programs including royalty, bedtime, bears, and things that go.

Carlson, Bernice Wells. *Listen! And Help Tell the Story*. il. by Burmah Burris. Nashville, Tenn.: Abingdon, 1965.

You'll refer again and again to this original, clever, and varied collection of well-written fingerplays, action verses, and poems with sound effects. These activities cover a variety of subjects from bees and penguins to robots and rabbits. There are nineteen fingerplays, with easy and clear directions that appear next to the line to which they refer. You'll want to use all of them, as well as the fourteen action verses that are also appropriate for four and five year olds. Many of the poems with sound effects can be shared with this age group too. The other material — action stories, stories with sound effects, poems with refrains, and poems with choruses — is best used with older children.

Cromwell, Liz, Dixie Hibner, and John R. Faitel, compilers. *Finger Frolics: Over 250 Fingerplays for Children from 3 Years*, rev. ed. il. by Joan Lockwood. Livonia, Mich.: Partner Press, 1983.

What distinguishes the fingerplays in this large, spiral-bound paperback from others is their contemporary sound. The language is not formal or dated, which is a drawback of some fingerplays. Many of the rhymes in this collection are meant to be instructive, and they are perhaps best used in a school rather than a library setting. The table of contents quickly leads you to poems and rhymes about home, seasons, animals, weather, and holidays among other subjects.

Debs, Sheila, ed. *Kidstuff: A Treasury of Early Childhood Enrichment Materials*. Lake Park, Fla.: GuideLines Press, Nov. 1981- .

Kidstuff describes itself as a "monthly by-mail treasury of programming ideas." Each multipaged pamphlet contains original material, as well as material from other sources, on one subject. Subjects have included families, the zoo, babies, friendship, nonsense stories, insects, and lions. The material is aimed at toddlers, preschoolers, and primary-grade children.

In particular, check out the ideas for flannel-board stories, creative dramatics, and puppet plays. You'll find clear, direct instructions and patterns to make and use puppets and flannel-board characters. Craft and activity ideas are well thought out, although some of them might be too time consuming for your story program.

Glazer, Tom. *Do Your Ears Hang Low? Fifty More Musical Fingerplays*. il. by Mila Lazarevich. Garden City, N.Y.: Doubleday, 1980.

Glazer, Tom. *Eye Winker, Tom Tinker, Chin Chopper*. il. by Ron Himler. Garden City, N.Y.: Doubleday, 1973.

Eye Winker, Tom Tinker, Chin Chopper is a delightful, illustrated collection that includes fifty familiar and unfamiliar musical fingerplays. Although piano arrangements and guitar chords are included, the songs and all their verses can be sung without accompaniment. The fingerplays can also be enjoyed by themselves. The author has included extremely explicit and lucid instructions for using them. You will not have to struggle to learn these fingerplays, and most are easy enough for preschoolers to execute.

Do Your Ears Hang Low?, the companion book to *Eye Winker*, shares the same excellent qualities. In it you can find other favorite musical fingerplays, including "Little Jack Horner," "London Bridge is Falling Down," "Over in the Meadow," and "Ten in a Bed."

Grayson, Marion F. *Let's Do Fingerplays*. il. by Nancy Weyl. Washington, D.C.: Robert B. Luce, 1962.

Some of the fingerplays in this book are dated, but most of them are still enjoyed by four and five year olds. "The World Outdoors" is a short section, but the fingerplays on the seasons are quite good. The collection is also a good source for Christmas and Halloween fingerplays and counting rhymes. Instructions for the actions follow each line of verse.

Hart, Jane, compiler. *Singing Bee! A Collection of Favorite Children's Songs*.
il. by Anita Lobel. New York: Lothrop, Lee & Shepard Books, 1982.

Lullabies, Mother Goose rhymes, fingerplays, singing games, folk songs,
holiday songs, and rounds are included in this collection of 125 songs. Most
are well-known, traditional titles; others are modern songs. Useful features are
the notes included for fingerplays and singing games and the song title and
subject indexes. The lively color and black-and-white illustrations by Anita
Lobel complement the songs and make this an exquisite and classic collection.

Hogstrom, Daphne. *Little Boy Blue: Finger Plays Old and New*. il. by Alice
Schlesinger. Racine, Wis.: Western Publishing, 1966.

Hogstrom, Daphne. *My Big Book of Fingerplays: A Fun-to-Say, Fun-to-Play
Collection*. il. by Sally Augustiny. Racine, Wis.: Western Publishing,
1974.

Hogstrom's books are oversized collections of fingerplays and action
rhymes. Sketches are used to indicate gestures and the written directions are
usually located near these sketches. Because the sketches and the written
directions aren't right next to the rhymes, it takes a bit longer to understand
how to do each activity. Don't let this or the uninspired illustrations put you
off. These activities are original, clever, and fun for children to do. The action
rhymes which dominate the collections are particularly liked by children.
These activities can be used in a wide range of programs, from sea and circus
to royalty and farms.

Hunt, Mary Alice, ed. *A Multimedia Approach to Children's Literature: A
Selective List of Films (and Videocassettes), Filmstrips and Recordings
Based on Children's Books*, 3d ed. Chicago: American Library Associa-
tion, 1983.

Use this book when you want to buy or borrow book-related, nonprint
material. This is a very selective collection arranged alphabetically by book
title. Each book title is followed by film, filmstrip, and record versions of the
book. You'll find helpful information, including brief annotations, age levels,
playing times, and comments on music and narrator when they are particularly
noteworthy. If you have a book that is too small to share with a group of
children, check this source to see if a quality film or filmstrip version exists.

Lima, Carolyn W. *A to Zoo: Subject Access to Children's Picture Books*, 2d
ed. New York: R. R. Bowker, 1986.

Lima's book is a comprehensive subject guide that lists book titles,
arranged alphabetically by author, within subject headings. A separate index
gives full bibliographic information for each book. Use this guide to lead you
to titles on a specific subject. You can also quickly determine whether there are
enough books to do a program on a subject you're considering. And, you
might see a book listed under a subject for which you never considered it. A
word of caution: Use this book as a starting point because titles included span
preschool through grade two. Without examining a specific title, you really
can't tell if it will work in a story hour or not.

Mother Goose. *Tomie dePaola's Mother Goose*. il. by Tomie dePaola. New
York: Putnam, 1985.

This is a beautifully illustrated collection of over 200 Mother Goose
rhymes. Many are well known; others are less familiar. You'll want to share

the full-color paintings filled with humor and playfulness with your story-hour group. Open your program with one of these poems; they fit into so many program subjects. Use your imagination, and turn some of these rhymes into fingerplays.

Olson, Margaret J. *Lots More Tell and Draw Stories*. Minneapolis, Minn.: Arts & Crafts Unlimited, 1973.

Olson, Margaret J. *More Tell and Draw Stories*. Minneapolis, Minn.: Arts & Crafts Unlimited, 1969.

Olson, Margaret J. *Tell and Draw Stories*. Minneapolis, Minn.: Creative Storytime Press, 1963.

These books are clever collections of original short stories that you can tell and create on a chalkboard or a large piece of paper. The table of contents shows an illustration of what your finished creation will be next to the accompanying story title. This tells you at a glance in what program you can use an item. Each story has step-by-step drawings on the left side of the page keyed to the text. You'll find them easy to learn and execute.

Peterson, Carolyn Sue, and Brenny Hall. *Story Programs: A Source Book of Materials*. Metuchen, N.J.: Scarecrow Press, 1980.

You'll find ideas for programming with toddlers, preschoolers, and primary-grade children in this book. The chapters on flannel-board activities, creative dramatics, and puppetry are particularly useful. You'll find songs, poems, and stories with patterns for use as flannel-board activities. In the puppetry chapter, you'll find verses, songs, stories, and plays to use with puppets. Patterns are included as well as direct instructions on how to make and work puppets.

In each chapter, check material for all age levels because some of the material in the sections devoted to toddlers and the primary level is appropriate to use with preschoolers.

Prelutsky, Jack, selector. *Read-Aloud Rhymes for the Very Young*. il. by Marc Brown. New York: Alfred A. Knopf, 1986.

This is an essential collection of poetry to use with story-hour-age children. It covers virtually every subject within a young child's experience and includes poems by all the fine poets. Many of the poems can be adapted as fingerplays or done on the felt board. The illustrations are soft, playful, and expressive. You'll want to share them with the children as you read the poems aloud.

The Raffi Singable Songbook: A Collection of 51 Songs from Raffi's First Three Records for Young Children. il. by Joyce Yamamoto. New York: Crown, 1987.

The 2nd Raffi Songbook. piano arrangements by Catherine Ambrose. design and illustration by Joyce Yamamoto. New York: Crown, 1986.

You'll want to share many of these lively and humorous songs with your story-hour group. Children and adults love them. Even if you can't read music, you can borrow the album from which the songs come and listen to them to learn the tune. The first collection has a "Songs by Album Index." In the second Raffi songbook the songs are arranged by album.

These songs fit into many story-hour categories including frogs, moon, friends, rain, gardening, and things that go.

Ring a Ring O'Roses: Stories, Games and Finger Plays for Pre-School Children, rev. ed. Flint, Mich.: Flint Public Library, 1981.

If you can only own one collection of fingerplays, purchase this small-format paperback. *Ring a Ring O' Roses* is probably the most comprehensive collection of its type. Over 450 fingerplays and action rhymes are divided by major headings and subheadings that are listed in the table of contents. Among the best sections are "Animal Kingdom," "Down on the Farm," "Holidays," "Child from Top to Toe," and "Things That Go." There are many counting rhymes that are quite appropriate for four and five year olds.

Sierra, Judy. *The Flannel Board Storytelling Book*. Chicago: H. W. Wilson, 1987.

This is a fine collection of thirty-six classic stories, poems, and songs to do on a felt board. The instructions and patterns are simple and can be embellished as you wish. The author includes instructions on how to move the pieces and where to place them. Follow-up activities are included for the stories.

Sutherland, Zena. *Children and Books*. 7th ed. Glenview, Ill.: Scott, Foresman, 1986.

This is a comprehensive text about children's books. If you're new at evaluating and selecting children's books, then read the chapters entitled "Books for the Very Young," "Artists and Children's Books," and "Poetry." These discussions and the bibliographies that follow will give you a basic foundation from which you can build your knowledge of children's books. Consult the appendix entitled "Book Selection Aids" for other useful titles.